Nolan Ryan's Pitcher's Bible

THE ULTIMATE GUIDE TO POWER, PRECISION, AND LONG-TERM PERFORMANCE

NOLAN RYAN AND TOM HOUSE
WITH JIM ROSENTHAL

A Fireside Book · Published by Simon & Schuster
New York London Toronto Sydney

Simon & Schuster/Fireside

Rockefeller Center
1230 Avenue of the Americas
New York, New York 10020

SIMON & SCHUSTER, FIRESIDE and colophon are
registered trademarks of Simon & Schuster, Inc.

Illustrations by Alison Cromwell
Photographs by Louis DeLuca
Designed by Bonni Leon
Manufactured in the United States of America

10 9 8 7 6 5 4 3 2 1
20   PBK

Library of Congress Cataloging in Publication Data
Ryan, Nolan, date
    [Pitcher's bible]
    Nolan Ryan's pitcher's bible : the ultimate guide to power,
precision, and long-term performance / Nolan Ryan and Tom House,
with Jim Rosenthal.
       p.   cm.
    "A Fireside book."
    1. Pitching (Baseball).   2. Ryan, Nolan, date.   I House, Tom.
II. Rosenthal, Jim.   III. Title: Pitcher's bible.
GV871.R95   1991
796.357'22—dc20   90-26518
                                                   CIP
ISBN 0-671-73709-0
    0-671-70581-4 (pbk)

Contents

Foreword: The Vanishing Fastball

A. Eugene Coleman, Ed.D.

It is ironic that Nolan Ryan can still throw a 95–97-mph fastball at age 43, while less than 7 percent of major-league pitchers are capable of throwing 90 mph at all, and average fastball velocity is decreasing by almost 2 mph per decade.

Why, when pitching is so important, is there a shortage of power pitchers? Velocity has decreased in baseball, to some extent, because young pitchers don't throw enough fastballs, pitches per workout, or pitches per week. Some professional scouts believe the problem begins in Little League. Young players realize that it's easier to trick hitters than to throw a fastball by them. The end result is a growing number of youngsters with good breaking balls and below-average velocity.

The trend for high school and college pitchers is similar: College pitchers today often throw 50 percent off-speed pitches, and the percentage is even higher in high school. I've charted several successful high school teams whose pitchers threw 60–65 percent off-speed pitches.

Many people in professional baseball point to aluminum bats as the source for changes in basic pitching patterns. The inside fastball, which almost always jams hitters using wooden bats, loses its effectiveness against an aluminum bat. Instead of throwing inside, then, pitchers spot their fastball and use their breaking ball as their out pitch. These young pitchers basically discard the fastball and do little to develop the strength and durability of their arms.

My encounters with both amateur and professional athletes indicate that throwing hard is a skill that can be improved with proper training and practice. The key word is *proper*. Training and practice, no matter how extensive, won't be effective unless they're directed specifically at the task at hand.

Some coaches believe that power pitchers are born, not developed. They contend that it's easier to teach a player to throw strikes than to teach him to throw hard, and so they spend more time trying to teach mechanics to players who throw hard than trying to get additional velocity out of pitchers with good mechanics.

But you can, within limits, teach someone to throw harder. While genetics determine someone's ultimate potential, improvement is possible with training.

Former Toronto pitcher Bill Caudill added to his throwing velocity after working with a javelin coach. Unlike baseball, where players with weak arms seldom improve, most javelin throwers increase distance by 10–15 feet per year. Distance and speed are related; you can't throw far if you can't throw hard, and vice versa. If track athletes can throw a two-pound javelin 10–15 feet farther after training, shouldn't we expect baseball players to throw a five-ounce ball farther and faster?

You can train to throw harder and faster, but not without a lot of work. Most of us never reach our true potential. Nolan, of course, is the exception because he followed the right path to take advantage of his natural skills. And that path begins with proper mechanics.

In the last decade, Nolan Ryan has thrown more than 100,000 pitches, with 65,000 clocked in the 90–100-mph range. Without proper mechanics, it would be impossible for Nolan to generate enough force to accelerate a baseball to 90 mph. Likewise, without good mechanics, he'd be unable to repeat these forces thousands of times without serious trauma to the arm and shoulder.

In his early years with the Angels, Nolan was encouraged to throw mostly fastballs. It was not unusual for him to throw 160–200 fastballs in an outing, a practice that many experts feel has helped him maintain a 90-mph fastball for more than 20 years. Today, it's almost unheard of for a pitcher to throw that many pitches of any kind. The current tendency of pitching coaches to limit the number of pitches thrown per game can hinder a young pitcher's ability to build adequate arm strength— the intangible element enabling a hurler to maximize his velocity over a long period of time.

In the past, pitchers became concerned with breaking balls and off-speed pitches only after their fastball began to slip. Today, however, youngsters are preoccupied with trick pitches. Gordon Goldsberry of the Baltimore Orioles estimates that two thirds of college hurlers are breaking-ball pitchers. No pitcher in the last three amateur drafts could throw as hard as Nolan does at 43.

You can't develop a good fastball by throwing off-speed pitches. Specificity of training dictates that you get what you train for. A sprinter who spends 80 percent of his time jogging is training to run slowly. A pitcher who throws 80 percent breaking balls is training to pitch at a slow velocity. You must use your fastball or lose it.

Young pitchers should aspire to throw harder, but never without a good base of conditioning. Lifting weights and running are tools to increase velocity, but only throwing can build the endurance required to hurl 100–150 pitches on a regular basis.

The Red Sox, White Sox, and Blue Jays have experimented with using a four-man rotation throughout their minor-league systems. The theory is that arm strength and velocity can be improved by throwing more times per week.

Al Rosen (San Francisco Giants) and Harry Dalton (Milwaukee Brewers) believe that young pitchers are underworked. Rosen says that coaches and managers are too protective of young arms, while Dalton points to the increasing number of pitchers disabled each year as a signal that something is wrong with conventional training procedures.

At the major-league level, where most pitchers are mechanically sound and throw at regular intervals, proper training often determines whether a pitcher's velocity is above or below the league average; inadequate training is often responsible for substandard velocity. Experience indicates that most pitchers with below-average velocity do not train properly.

I have had the opportunity to know and work with both Nolan Ryan and Tom House for more than a decade. Their knowledge of conditioning, mechanics, and the mental aspects of baseball is unrivaled. Their approach to the game is based on scientific principles and proven major-league practice. I recommend this book to players of all ages and ability levels.

Dr. Coleman is director of conditioning for the Houston Astros.

●

FOREWORD

●

Nolan Ryan's Pitcher's Bible

My Physical Education

When I signed back in 1965, the standard approach to training for pitching was quite simple: Just throw off a mound, do some sprints, and you're all set.

Based on the information available in the 1960s, this training program wasn't too far off-course. A pitcher has to have really strong legs, naturally. And you do need to get used to throwing off a mound to get your arm in shape and build up your stamina.

As for spring training, my goal (which was also shared by the coaching staff) was to add to my leg strength and notch 25–35 innings in exhibition play. If I got that done, then I felt I was ready to start the season.

This was a sound policy for its time. But as I would learn, it did not deal with a lot of the strength-deficiency problems that haunt pitchers, and it wasn't an adequate way to prepare for a long season, when you're going to pitch 250 or 300 innings.

I first ran up against the fragile nature of a pitcher's life in 1967. I had just come out of the service—I'd been on active duty for six months—and the Mets sent me to Florida to prepare for the major-league campaign.

I was in pretty decent shape, but in no condition to throw at full speed. As soon as I arrived at Jacksonville, Florida, I started overextending myself, going full tilt before I was physically ready to pitch. My forearm tightened. I kept throwing, but then—sure enough—I felt something pop. A tendon popped in my forearm in much the same way a rubber band snaps if you stretch it too far.

I really thought my career was over. I figured I'd be back in Alvin, Texas, doing something besides playing baseball for a living. In those days, if you hurt your arm they didn't have elaborate surgical procedures, and there were no sports-medicine clinics for extended rehabilitation. If your arm didn't heal, you were through.

After the injury, I returned to Alvin to rest my arm all summer. I couldn't even throw a ball three feet, let alone pitch. My only option was to let nature take its course and hope for the best. I didn't have the ranch in Alvin or my cattle business yet, so it wasn't easy to work off my frustration—I couldn't even play tennis.

But that summer did have its pleasures. Ruth, my high school sweetheart, and I got married, my arm got the rest it needed, and eventually it healed enough to enable me to look forward to the 1968 season.

During the next four years with the Mets (1968–71), my conditioning program was pretty much identical to the other pitchers, a group that included Tom Seaver, Jerry Koosman, and Gary Gentry. Rube Walker, our pitching coach, had our pitchers run every day, except for the guy who was slated to start that night. We'd run during the last 20 minutes of batting practice, and then maybe throw on the sidelines. We didn't do any distance-throwing or long toss.

Rube was a very perceptive coach. He had a good eye for when his pitchers were tiring and needed to come out of the game, and he knew each guy's delivery well enough to pinpoint flaws that could lead to arm trouble.

Unfortunately, because of the military obligations I had while with the Mets, I never got a chance to pitch enough innings to be consistent. My wildness made it hard for the Met organization to have patience with me. And this prompted my trade to the Angels prior to the 1972 season.

I looked at the trade as a new lease on life. The Angels were going through a rebuilding phase, and I felt that if I could go to California and have a strong spring I'd win a starting spot. Here was my chance to pitch a lot of innings and finally prove I could do the job.

Now, I don't know if I tried to do too much or what, but I had a miserable spring camp. I thought I might have blown my opportunity to make the starting rotation. But I didn't give up

on myself. I started the third or fourth game—it was against the Minnesota Twins—and pitched a shutout. This really helped me secure a position in the rotation—just the break I needed.

The 1972 season was a transitional point in my career; it was the year I started lifting weights. The Angels had a Universal gym in an obscure back room at Anaheim Stadium—a far cry from the way major-league teams now offer state-of-the-art weight facilities in the clubhouse. In those days, of course, it was unheard of for a pitcher to train with weights. But I felt that there had to be more a pitcher could do to maintain his stamina and strengthen his upper body; by using weights I believed I'd be a better-conditioned athlete. So I basically just started lifting, experimenting with different exercises to see what kind of results I'd get.

When I embarked on my lifting adventure I was working out on a typical 12-station Universal gym. It had most of the basic machines: bench press, military press, and leg extension, to name a few. I followed a balanced program rather than just concentrating on my upper or lower body. If I had any emphasis at that point it was probably on my legs; remember, I had no guidelines on what I should be doing for my upper body, and there was a great fear among old-line baseball people then that weight lifting would make you musclebound. I just sort of felt my way through it and listened to what my body was telling me.

I structured my lifting around the four-man rotation; I'd train the first two days after pitching and then recover on the third. Obviously, my goal was to lift heavy enough to gain strength, but not so heavy as to make me stiff or sore.

Then I made an important discovery. I found that even if I was somewhat stiff from lifting, it really had no effect on my ability to pitch. And after I began using the weights consistently, my arm would bounce back more quickly from one start to the next.

I was so pleased with these results that I bought a Universal gym and installed it in my house. It was not only a more convenient arrangement, but also the perfect excuse for continuing with my weight training after the 1972 campaign came to an

end. My off-season regimen included lifting Mondays, Wednesdays, and Fridays, while also doing a fair share of running and stretching.

Bob Anderson, hired by the Angels as a stretching instructor in 1974, really influenced my thinking on flexibility and endurance. Bob taught me a lot about stretching, how it could warm up the muscles and prevent injuries. He was also an advocate of long-distance running for pitchers. I worked up to five miles a day and sustained that routine for a couple of years until my knees and back started bothering me.

Since I couldn't run often enough, I began doing some of my cardiovascular work on the stationary bike. During the season,

of course, I always structure my cardio training around the rotation. When I was with the Angels and pitching in a four-man rotation, for instance, I'd try to do my distance-running the first and second days after pitching, take a day off, and then pitch the next day. But in Texas, where we adhere to a five-man rotation, I perform my lifting on the first and third days and usually ride the bike the first three days after a start.

One of the keys to my success with the Angels was that my velocity actually increased in the later innings. Now, this skill certainly could be attributed to establishing a rhythm, finding a good groove, and improving my mechanics as the game went along. But the conditioning program made this possible by increasing my stamina. Once you fatigue, it affects your mechanics; you can no longer pitch with the precise timing required for a smooth, compact motion.

The conditioning regimen definitely paid dividends for my endurance. During my first three years in the American League I pitched more than 900 innings, a surefire formula for ending up with a strength deficit. There's no way I could have recovered as quickly, or been as durable, without a firm base of strength from lifting.

My weight routine didn't add velocity to my fastball per se; I think velocity has more to do with rhythm and mechanics. But the weights gave me the opportunity to be more consistent.

While I was lifting weights and striking guys out in Anaheim, Tom House was lifting weights and getting into a heap of trouble in Atlanta. Tom's manager, Eddie Mathews, even told him he'd be sent to the minor leagues if he continued his weight training.

Tom and I didn't know each other in the 1970s, but I can understand what he was going through. Management simply did not want pitchers fooling around with Universal machines or dumbbells. I knew how they felt and so I didn't broadcast the fact I was into a weight program.

But Tom's situation was different. He'd always been a maverick, the kind of guy who was extremely outspoken. And, unfortunately, he wasn't held in very high esteem by the Braves organization; he'd departed from the accepted training standards of baseball and was forced to pay the price.

Part of Tom's problem was that he was building some visible bulk. He's probably 20–30 pounds lighter now than he was in those days. If he knew then what he knows now about diet and exercise, I'm sure he would have developed into a better-conditioned athlete.

Tom and I both worked for the Houston Astros organization in 1980, but we didn't really have any contact with each other. I was pitching in the big leagues; Tom was a minor-league instructor. I don't think he even knew about my commitment to conditioning and weight training. But we shared a common source of valuable information on diet, training, and nutrition: Gene Coleman, the Astros' strength-and-conditioning instructor.

Gene, a professor of human performance at the University of Houston, Clear Lake, inspired Tom to pursue his own research on exercises specific to pitching. As for me, well, let's just say that Gene is the person who fine-tuned my program to better address my needs as a power pitcher.

Gene began by adding the Jobe light-dumbbell program to my repertoire. In the earliest days of my trial-and-error lifting, there was little or no information about strengthening the rotator cuff and shoulder capsule through exercise. Dr. Frank Jobe developed his light-dumbbell program to eliminate the serious, career-ending shoulder injuries then plaguing pitchers.

Collaborating with Gene was a turning point in my career; I became more familiar with the principles of throwing a baseball and better equipped to prevent the discomfort and injuries that result from mechanical inefficiency.

Right after I signed with the Astros, Gene took me on a tour of the weight room—a complete Nautilus setup consisting of about 20 machines—and he demonstrated how to use the equipment to satisfy my strength requirements. I continued to perform many of the lower-body exercises from my days with the Angels, but added new Nautilus movements for the upper body.

Abdominal exercise was—and is—one of my greatest concerns. Baseball players rarely did much for the midsection, but I always treated it as a priority. Gene and I agreed that you generate force with your legs and apply it with your arms, but

the energy must be transferred through the trunk—it's a three-link chain, and the chain is only as strong as its weakest link.

If you don't focus on ab training, then you'll be unable to transfer the energy efficiently through the midsection and more stress will be placed on the arm.

Another reason to work your midsection is to prevent lower-back injuries. A lot of people don't understand how essential the abdominal muscles are in providing support for the lower back. I always knew ab training was important, and Gene helped to reinforce its urgency.

A real stroke of luck for me was that the strength programs favored by Gene in Houston and Tom in Arlington are quite compatible. Though the Astros don't emphasize free weights and heavy dumbbells as much as Tom does with Texas Rangers pitchers, both teams essentially share the same workout philosophy.

When I signed with the Rangers prior to the 1989 season, I made a point of contacting Tom to discuss his program. I wanted to assure him that I wasn't going to come in and create problems. I'm always open to new information. I listen to what someone has to say and see if it can be applied to what I do; if it's not of any value, then I won't use it.

I pretty much went along with everything Tom was doing. He was recommending exercises that did more for developing the back side of the shoulder (rear deltoid). This is an area where a pitcher tends to develop a deficit, because there are three muscle groups that accelerate the arm but only two muscle groups that decelerate it. Tom understands the workload you expend throwing a baseball and what it takes in the weight room to compensate for the strength you lose while pitching. That kind of information is very helpful and beneficial.

Tom refined my program to balance muscle strength, both from front to back and from right to left. I believe in balancing strength; you need to train both sides of the body evenly and symmetrically. Just because you throw right-handed doesn't mean you can ignore your left side. Your left side is, in fact, as important to throwing a baseball properly as your right side; lack

of strength in the left half of your trunk—basically a muscle imbalance—will put undue strain on your stronger side when you're delivering the baseball.

Tom's ideas and exercise principles were fine. My problem had more to do with understanding just what he was talking about. I'm used to describing things in layman's terms, while Tom tends to express his ideas in more technical language. When we would sit down to discuss an exercise, he'd give me his explanation, and then I'd sort through what he said to make sure we were on the same wavelength.

Take throwing a football to improve mechanics. We discussed the benefits of tossing a perfect spiral, how it rehearses the correct mechanical motion of a pitcher's delivery. Tom says you can't throw a perfect spiral without perfect mechanics, so throwing the football gives you a check on yourself. But I didn't want to rush into anything. I chose to wait until my arm was in shape before giving it a try. Once the season began, I started throwing the football around as part of my warm-up. The results were good—it's really beneficial to mechanics—so I incorporated it into my pre-game ritual.

The elastic-cord program for pitchers, an isometric exercise regimen designed to enhance range of motion, is the one component of Tom's program that I don't do. The cord isolates the tendon in my elbow that was injured in 1986. I feel like I have some scar tissue in there—it's a sensitive area. Naturally, I'm not going to take a chance on hurting myself. But I'm an exception. The cord program belongs in a pitcher's workout plan; anything you can do to increase range of motion is a plus.

Right now, I'm essentially plugged into the same program as the other Rangers pitchers. I work on building a base of muscle strength in the off-season—weight training Mondays, Wednesdays, and Fridays—and then in-season I lift about 70 percent of maximum poundage on the first and third days following a start.

The biggest challenge is finding enough time to exercise. A lot of people work upper body one day and lower body the next. That's fine, but I don't have the luxury of performing a split workout, because I have to have my whole body in synch on that fifth day. So I'll circuit-train—work the whole body in one exercise session—to get through the program in 90 minutes to two hours. Then I'll rest the following day, allowing me to come back even stronger when it's my turn to pitch.

Enjoying success requires the ability to adapt. You shouldn't outline a program and then etch it in stone. We all have different physical limitations and skills that make us unique individuals. Try to make modifications in your program to enhance it; that's always been my approach. If something can help you, then give it a chance. Only by being open to change will you have a true opportunity to get the most from your God-given talent.

Mental
Discipline

2

Being able to adapt to changing circumstances has helped me tremendously—it has been one of the keys to my success. When I first came up from the minors, for example, I'd dare a hitter to try to handle my fastball. I applied the mentality of a gunfighter to my craft. A guy either had the skill and timing to hit the heater or he struck out.

I don't really think of myself as a gunfighter anymore. The fastball is still my bread-and-butter pitch, and I'll go with it in crucial situations. But I'm much more conscious of location. That's the biggest difference between the Nolan Ryan of 15–20 years ago and the Nolan Ryan of today.

Check my minor-league stats and you'll see I was either striking everyone out or walking them. I had the kind of velocity— 98 mph with regularity—that allowed me the luxury of not being so fine with my control. Well, those days couldn't last forever. I now throw 93, 94 mph—still fast, but not overpowering enough to base all my success on blowing guys away.

I worked long and hard to master the control of my breaking ball and change-up. As my confidence in those pitches improved, I was able to set hitters up, get ahead in the count, and apply strategy instead of sheer force.

Control of the curve and change-up transformed me from being only a fastball thrower to more of a tactical pitcher. I've heard some people say that going to the National League made me a complete pitcher because I couldn't just rely on my fastball. Well, nothing happened in my head to make the change—that's just a bunch of hogwash. Ten years after I came back to the National League, I'm still getting hitters out with my fastball. If you fall behind in the count you still have to throw your best pitch—and for me that's the fastball.

It requires incredible concentration to get the location I want on every fastball. I can't let up—*even for a second.* Mental discipline and intense focus on what you're doing begins early in a pitcher's day. Before each start I sit in the clubhouse and analyze the other team's hitters. I concentrate on visualizing what I've done in the past to get a hitter out, consider his strengths and weaknesses. I just sort of run through the lineup in my mind; it's a pre-game ritual that reinforces the fact that I'm mentally prepared to pitch effectively.

Once the game gets going, though, all that planning is subject to change. Maybe I can't throw the breaking ball for strikes. Some days it's not going to break as much as I'd expected. Well, I simply have to adjust by throwing more fastballs and change-ups. This is where a lot of young pitchers run into trouble—

they're unable to adjust and end up losing their concentration as soon as things take a turn for the worse.

I don't use any particular gimmicks or fancy techniques to enhance my concentration. I just block things out, focusing completely on the task of retiring the hitter. Maintaining concentration depends on what I call tunnel vision; nothing else in the world exists but the catcher's target, the hitter, and my perfect delivery. This is a space where I feel comfortable and relaxed. I don't get distracted by all the external stuff going on around me.

The ability to block things out is something you develop through experience. Young pitchers have a tendency to lose their composure on the mound, falling prey to negative thoughts. Tom Seaver and Jerry Koosman were notable exceptions; they were both blessed with incredible mental discipline. The entire Mets' staff, in fact, was remarkable for its mental maturity.

Unfortunately, some pitchers are unable to learn how to concentrate and focus properly. I've played with very talented athletes who never appreciated how important the mental side of baseball is to success; not surprisingly, most of them didn't last too long, even though they had enough talent to win ball games.

You can't have a long, successful career without a positive attitude. I believe that an I-can-do-this mentality is a pitcher's best friend. You must have confidence in your stuff. That confidence translates into an aggressive—not arrogant—posture on the mound. (Blatant arrogance, such as staring a guy down, is unprofessional and makes the hitter even more determined to beat you at your own game.) A pitcher lacking in self-confidence, however, can't be aggressive, and that timidity will betray you every time.

It's easy to identify pitchers who are afraid of getting hit hard; they lose confidence in their fastball so they won't throw it for strikes, they nibble and get behind in the count. What these pitchers don't realize is that they're beating themselves. Trying to be too fine, they lose their edge and are forced to pitch defensively. A pitcher with the count in his favor has the advantage. Once you get ahead on the hitter, then you've got all your options and you can throw your best stuff. If you make a bad pitch in that spot you've got no one but yourself to blame.

Throwing inside to a hitter is at the heart of aggressive pitching. You can't let the fear of hitting—or hurting—the hitter deter you from coming in with a fastball. Of course, it's essential to have confidence in your control and in your ability to throw inside. But don't let your concern over hitting somebody and putting him on base take away from your aggressiveness. If you teach a hitter that you'll throw inside—if he knows that—then his whole approach to facing you is quite different.

A lot of young pitchers in the big leagues right now are afraid to throw inside. This fear invites a hitter to dig in and dominate the outer part of the plate. The decline of the inside pitch can be traced to two factors: a lack of instruction at the minor-league level, and the recent rule changes discouraging guys from coming in too often—umpire warnings, for instance, that lead to pitchers getting kicked out of the game. Umpires should have the power to prevent beanball wars, ugly incidents where players get hurt and things get out of hand. But I've also seen umpires warn pitchers in cases that didn't warrant it, where a strategic inside pitch got away from someone who wasn't trying to hit anybody.

Pitching inside was a fact of life in the 1960s. You had to demonstrate early in the game that you were more than happy to pitch in to a hitter to keep him honest. In an 0–2 situation it was taken for granted that you'd come in on a hitter to make your pitches away more effective.

Young pitchers have to realize that it's okay to claim the inside part of the plate as their own. It's especially important these days, what with hitters having the advantage of using aluminum

bats at the college level. Those aluminum bats make a pitcher's life even harder. For one thing, a guy can fist out a hit without making solid contact; a broken-bat foul ball with wood is often a single with aluminum. But you still have to establish that you're not afraid to pitch inside. You can't afford to let a hitter develop a comfort zone. If he knows you won't throw in, then he'll dive out over the plate. You have to put the thought in his mind that you're willing to pitch in—always keep the hitter guessing. Never show your hand. I talked to my son Reid, a freshman at the University of Texas, about pitching in and I explained to him that discretion is the key to this technique: If you throw a fastball inside, you're occasionally going to hit a batter. Well, you certainly don't want to nail a guy with men on base when you could lose a ball game because of it. So, in a do-or-die situation, always consider how good your control is before throwing inside to a hitter.

Control determines your effectiveness—whether you're pitching inside or outside. It's really a double-edged sword. When you pitch inside and your location is off, well, two things can happen: either you hit the guy (missing inside) or throw the ball right over the heart of the plate (missing outside). But you run the same risk pitching to the outer half of the plate—too far out and it's a wild pitch; too far in and the hitter gets a good pitch to drive.

If you do have enough control to throw to both sides of the plate, though, pitching inside will increase the effectiveness of your outside pitches and give you more of the outer part of the strike zone to work with. You don't want a hitter leaning over the plate, anticipating that you're going to throw the ball where he wants it.

Of course, some hitters don't like the outside pitch. This is especially true of righthanded hitters who have short arms and a compact swing. But tall righthanders prefer the ball out over the plate—they just extend their arms to make contact. And

•

MENTAL DISCIPLINE

•

lefthanders look for the ball over the middle, generally down and in. All hitters have their distinct strengths and weaknesses. You can't generalize about a hitter's favorite pitch—just believe in your ability to get the guy with your best stuff. Don't compromise. It's your move; you have to be the aggressor or you'll lose that mental edge.

Getting ahead in the count is the key to being a winning pitcher. If you can throw strikes right from the get-go, then it makes your job so much easier. Most hitters lose confidence and alter their style in a 1–2 or 0–2 situation. (Wade Boggs is the exception; he'd rather hit with two strikes because it helps him to concentrate, and Wade says he has a better grasp of the strike zone with an 0–2 count. But guys like Boggs are few and far between.)

I like to get ahead of a hitter by starting him off away, especially if it's the first time I've faced him in that particular game. My theory is that you pitch in when you're ahead in the count, and pitch outside when you're behind. Say I have a 2–1 count on Dave Winfield. In that spot Dave is going to look for a ball to pull, something he can drive into the gap in left-center or smack over the fence. So I'll throw the pitch—whether it's a fastball or curve—on the outside of the plate to neutralize his power. If I'm ahead 1–2, though, he'll just want to protect the plate and be more likely to look for a pitch away—that's the perfect time to bust him inside. Is Winfield guessing fastball or curve in this situation? Well, my pitch selection—and what Winfield expects me to throw—depends on so many variables: Am I throwing my breaking ball for strikes? What did he do in his last at bat against me? All of our experience with each other goes into these decisions.

Let's say I mess up and Dave hits a long home run over the center-field fence in Arlington Stadium. I can't let the failure of that last pitch to Winfield affect the success of my next pitch

to Dante Bichette, Lance Parrish, or whoever is batting behind Dave in the Angels' lineup.

You see young pitchers struggle with this type of situation all the time. One guy gets a rally going with a double ripped down the line. Then, before you know it, the pitcher who gave up the double refuses to throw the ball over the plate, or won't throw that pitch again at all. If you go back and analyze it, the pitch that was tagged was probably a mistake; the pitcher gave his opponent something to hit instead of making a quality pitch to a good location. But if you have confidence in yourself, you'll know those mistakes are the exception rather than the rule, and you'll let yourself make that quality pitch the next time instead of blocking your own success with negative thoughts.

In game five of the 1986 playoffs, for instance, I tossed Darryl Strawberry of the New York Mets a low fastball and he smashed it for a home run to tie the game. Yeah, the pitch was in a good location, down and in. But it was a 3–2 fastball. Strawberry knew that in a one-run game I wouldn't want to walk him, so Darryl was confident that he'd see a fastball. And being a good fastball hitter, he took the best pitch I had to offer, made solid contact, and hit it out of the park.

Now, I can't lose confidence in my fastball just because Darryl Strawberry hit a home run off of it. I had to analyze the game situation and realize that he hit a home run because of his conviction that he was going to get a fastball. If I threw him a change-up for a strike he probably would have swung and missed, but I couldn't take a chance on walking him; if you walk a guy to start off an inning, then the whole way the game is played changes in a hurry. The opposing team has all sorts of options for advancing the base runner into scoring position, and before you know it you're playing catch-up.

If it seems as if everything is going against you (and this happens to the best of us), just step off the mound, take a deep breath, and think about what you're doing—allow yourself

•

**MENTAL
DISCIPLINE**

•

39

enough time to regroup. I really believe in that. Don't get so wrapped up in the emotional end of things that you lose direction; remember, never let the failure of your last pitch affect the success of your next one.

You should treat the art of pitching as you would a Thanksgiving dinner. Families get together for the holidays and there's always a lot of good food to enjoy. You're not going to eat everything at once, of course; a satisfying meal is best appreciated one bite at a time. Pitching a ball game is based on the same principle—deal with one pitch at a time and make every one count. Are the bases loaded with nobody out? That's fine; you still need to feel like there's no one on base. Just relax and make quality pitches, or your worst fears will come true.

Of course, the score of the game will influence my overall strategy. With a substantial lead, for instance, I'll just throw fastballs, keep the pitches down and let them put the ball in play. In a tight game, though, I'll be finer with my control and change speeds more. But the one thing that remains constant is my overall mental attitude: I just focus on getting ahead in the count and maintaining my composure.

If I can't work my way out of trouble and I do give up a run, then it's essential to cut it off right there. You can't fret over the fact that you've fallen behind in the game, given up a key run, or made a bad pitch; what's done is done. You have to look at it from the standpoint that it's your job to pitch effectively, regardless of the circumstances.

A lot of young pitchers even lose their confidence and their composure if their stuff isn't up to par in the bull pen. They'll take the mound with uncertainty, get depressed by the fact that they're not throwing well, and undermine any chance of being effective.

My advice is to see what you have and try to establish your pitches early in the game. If your curve isn't breaking or you

can't throw it for strikes, then make the necessary adjustments in your pitch selection. But you have to pitch every game differently; vary your repertoire as you see fit based on the stuff you've got on that particular day.

And never put too much stock in how you throw in the bull pen; loosening up your arm is not the same as pitching in a game. Here's proof: Right before I tossed my first no-hitter with the Angels, I was warming up in the bull pen and my stuff was simply horrendous. I couldn't find the plate, had poor velocity, and—to make matters worse—my curveball was flat. I honestly didn't think I'd get out of the first inning. I struggled with my control early on, but persisted until I found my rhythm and got into a good groove. By the end of the night I was throwing as well as I ever had.

This is an extreme but pertinent example of the fact that you don't predetermine in the bull pen how you're going to pitch in the game. I've seen pitchers warm up and just be absolutely overpowering, only to lose their concentration once they took the field. You can have great stuff, but it won't guarantee success until you understand—and master—the mental side of pitching.

Going after my 300th win was a real mental ordeal—an exercise in staying calm and controlled under unusual and difficult circumstances. I was hoping to get it done at home, what with all my friends and family in Arlington for the occasion. But, unfortunately, my first shot at win number 300 came against the Yankees, a team with a bunch of guys I'd never seen before. That made it tough. And the fact that I didn't have a good command of my fastball that night made it even tougher.

Before the game, I went over the Yankee lineup—really not knowing how to approach most of the hitters—and decided to prepare myself mentally for the few guys I'd pitched against in the past. Steve Sax was about the only one I had a good fix on: He's a fastball hitter who likes the ball up. My strategy was to

●

**MENTAL
DISCIPLINE**

●

41

keep him off-balance by throwing breaking stuff and fastballs down and away.

Again, a good pitcher has to adjust his strategy to suit the unique situations that present themselves during each game, each at bat. Here's how I dealt with Sax in pursuit of my 300th win:

In the first inning, with Deion Sanders at third base, I threw Sax three consecutive breaking balls. Falling behind 2–1, I came back with a low change-up for a strike to even the count. At 2–2, then, it was time for the low-and-away fastball. The problem was that my location was off—the pitch was out over the plate—and I ended up giving him a pretty good pitch to hit. With Deion at third, Sax was just trying to make contact to drive in the run, and his groundball out did just that.

In the third inning, while Deion was stealing second, I gave Sax a fastball up in the strike zone—definitely not where I wanted it. Fortunately, though, Sax took a big swing, missed, and fell behind in the count. I followed with a low breaking ball for a strike. And at 0–2, I went to the change-up—he blooped it to Steve Buechele at deep third for an infield hit.

In retrospect, the 0–2 change-up was a bad pitch. Sax was in a hole, just trying to put the ball in play and protect the plate. I gave him a pitch—a change on the fists—that he could fight off for a hit. A good breaking ball would have struck him out or forced him to hit a weak groundball instead of a bloop single.

Next time up—in the fifth inning—I decided to open with a fastball. I'd been struggling with my location on this pitch, but it's still my bread and butter. Sax took the fastball for a strike, 0–1. I threw him an inside curve, one that missed by a mile, and then retired him on a low curve that he grounded to Jeff Huson at shortstop. I stuck with the curve instead of going to the change because it was getting the job done.

In Steve's final at bat against me in the seventh inning, I threw him two low-and-away fastballs and he was retired (on

the second pitch) on a liner to Pete Incaviglia in left. The original strategy of low and outside fastballs worked the fourth time around; my problem on this night was that my location wasn't up to par, forcing me to counter with a diet of low breaking balls and one change-up I lived to regret.

I think the ability to respond in a positive way to failure is what sets winners apart from losers. I made a few bad pitches to Sax, but next time I'll know better and make the necessary adjustments for success.

Eddie Stanky deserves some credit for my understanding of the mental side of baseball. He stressed the importance of keeping your head in the game, how you can pick up little things about a hitter just by analyzing his stance—whether a guy is crowding the plate or backing away gives you a signal that he's making certain adjustments against you. Analysis is an important part of baseball. Here's a good example: Phil Niekro of the Atlanta Braves made a living off of his late-breaking knuckleball. The Astro hitters studied Niekro's delivery in pursuit of the ideal strategy: By moving up in the batter's box, they had a better shot at connecting with the pitch before it could break out of the hitting zone. Hitters know how to adapt; a smart pitcher is equally perceptive. I'm always evaluating a hitter's stance for more information.

There's more to pitching than just heading out to the mound and throwing strikes. All hitters—even the great ones—have their weaknesses. It's up to a pitcher to discover and exploit a hitter's flaws.

Unlike a lot of pitchers, I don't keep a written book on hitters; I work more on recollection. Is he a fastball hitter? Does he wait on the curve? Will he swing at the first pitch? All this information is filed away in my memory, ready and waiting to be put to the test of competition.

●

MENTAL DISCIPLINE

●

43

During the very brief exhibition season of 1990, I made the mistake of giving up a long home run to Sammy Sosa of the White Sox. I played with him in 1989—he was traded by the Rangers for Harold Baines—so I knew about his strengths and weaknesses. Sosa is an excellent fastball hitter, but not the most selective guy in the American League. My plan was to start him off with a fastball low and outside, but the pitch got away from me and he turned on it. I wanted to throw him a curve on the second pitch—but the home run took care of that idea in a real hurry.

I guess you could say I made a mistake by throwing the fastball on the first pitch. I knew Sosa would be guessing fastball, but if the pitch had been down and away—as I intended—he's lunging for the ball and it's strike, or out, number one. Location is everything in this situation. In a spring-training game I'm not going to have the precise control I need to apply ideal strategy to each at bat. But a pitcher can outthink the hitter if he's able to put the ball where he wants it—and he knows the batter's weak spots.

Quality hitters are hard to outthink. The guys I struggle against tend to wait back on the ball and just put it in play. Here are the contact hitters who have given me all kinds of trouble at various points in my career:

New York Mets

1—Matty Alou
2—Billy Williams
3—Pete Rose

California Angels

1—Rod Carew
2—Tony Oliva
3—George Brett

Houston Astros

1—Pete Rose
2—Will Clark
3—Tony Gwynn

Texas Rangers

1—Wade Boggs
2—Don Mattingly

These guys are all selective hitters with a vast knowledge of the strike zone—and are 10 of the most intense individuals you'd ever want to meet. In the final analysis, the mental aspect of baseball is as important to your success as your physical tools.

●

**MENTAL
DISCIPLINE**

●

Mechanics

Tom House has dedicated his professional baseball life to decoding the puzzle of perfect mechanics. His company, Bio-Kinetics, Inc., prepares detailed assessments of pitching technique through high-speed video recording and computerized motion analysis. As pitching coach with the Texas Rangers, Tom applies scientific principles to the real-world dilemma of retiring hitters like Wade Boggs and George Brett on a daily basis. Tom and I often discuss and analyze pitching mechanics during the

My starting position: comfortable, loose, ready.

The windup begins with a step back, arms lifted behind my head.

course of a long summer of baseball. Here are Tom's comments on the elements of mechanical precision.

The pitching motion is a study in control, with all parts moving in sequence to maximize the ability to throw a baseball. Let's visualize a pitcher who applies proper mechanics to his delivery:

He places both feet on the rubber, ball hidden inside the glove, as he keeps his eyes on the catcher's target. He initiates the

The high leg lift is a Nolan Ryan trademark, a key to generating power.

My critical checkpoint: leg lift at shoulder height, stance closed.

MECHANICS

windup by transferring his weight to the back foot with a small reverse or side step while comfortably lifting his hands as high as they'll go. He lifts—not kicks—his front knee up to its maximum height as the hands return to his center of gravity, somewhere on a line between chin and belly-button level. Then he begins a controlled fall toward home plate: the foot comes down in a steplike motion; his whole front side—glove, elbow, shoulder, hip, knee, and foot—is pointing toward home plate. His

As I move forward in a controlled fall, my hands separate and I prepare to hit the mound with my lead leg.

My foot on the ground, my shoulders and hips are just beginning to open up to deliver the ball.

hands break from the glove as the weight is transferred in a forward direction. As the landing leg hits the mound, the throwing arm attains its optimal launch position—both elbows are at shoulder height—then, the upper body delivers the arm and the arm delivers the baseball.

It's poetry in motion; a successful pitcher puts all the sequential phases of a delivery together so easily that the average fan sees only a fraction of what's actually taking place. But every

The upper body delivers my arm, and my arm delivers the ball.

The ball delivered, the legs, back, and shoulders absorb the force of decelerating the arm.

piece of the puzzle must fit together in perfect unity. Proper mechanics don't materialize overnight; they're a byproduct of hard work and adhering to the four essential elements of pitching: balance, direction, deception/launch, and weight transfer.

BALANCE Quite simply, balance is a pitcher's ability to stabilize his center of gravity. You have to position your body to direct all your energy straight toward home plate. There's no angular momentum, nothing to throw you off-course.

Ideal balance is the same for every pitcher. The balance point occurs when you lift your leg to its maximum height and your hands are aligned at the center of gravity—between chin and belly button. Ideally, hand and glove are just above the lift knee at this stage. Your head is directly over your pivot foot.

You want your posture as tall as possible. The taller you are in the balance position, the more angle downward in the trajectory of the ball you'll have at the release point—and the harder it will be for the hitter to see the pitch.

DIRECTION Once you achieve optimal balance, begin a controlled fall toward home plate, your front foot leading the way. Your hands will break naturally; turn your thumbs under to force your elbows up into launching position. Your entire front side—glove, elbow, shoulder, hip, knee, and foot—should be perfectly directional and on line with home plate. There's no rotation of the torso yet, no violent movements to displace ideal direction.

Think of the body as a gate that moves together as a single unit—no part of the gate should fly open as you advance toward home plate. If a pitcher opens up—hips rotating out toward first or third base—he'll place undue stress on the throwing arm while limiting the efficiency and power of the delivery.

DECEPTION/LAUNCH *These two components work in tandem. Your throwing and front-side elbows will both attain shoulder height at the launch phase. Let your forearms and hands form a 90-degree angle (in relation to upper arm) to maximize arm strength and leverage. The forearm, wrist, and glove on your front side, if they're properly aligned, will impede the hitter's view of your pitching arm in its launch position—this is the deceptive element of the equation. That front arm will delay the hitter's picking up your release point. (This is a common trait of pitchers considered "sneaky-fast.")*

WEIGHT TRANSFER *This intangible of mechanics is accomplished in a few distinct stages. Once your throwing elbow leads the throwing arm forward, your strong side replaces the directional side as weight is transferred to the landing leg. Your shoulders pass each other in opposite directions. Your head stays directly over the bent knee of your landing leg—again, to maximize leverage.*

Here is what happens at the release point: Your throwing arm—and wrist—snaps straight to full extension, then the palm rotates the thumb down and out, away from the body, as the ball leaves the fingertips. At this precise moment all acceleration ends and deceleration begins. Weight transfer is completed as your head and upper body are pulled past the knee of your landing leg. This final coup de grace allows the forces of deceleration to be transferred from the arm, through the upper torso, into the lower back and finally to the legs, rather than compelling the shoulder to bear the brunt of resistance.

A 200-pound pitcher generates 1,200 pounds of force when the landing leg strikes. A mechanically efficient hurler—one who understands the four essentials of pitching—translates that energy up through the entire upper body. If, however, you rush your delivery, spin out of direction or fail to transfer your weight properly, then you're a likely candidate for stiffness and soreness in the rear deltoid area.

The other common injuries tied to mechanical inefficiency are a tender elbow or strained front deltoid (shoulder) muscle. These ailments are often the result of drifting toward home plate while lifting the leg (before it reaches its apex) or rotating toward third or first base during the controlled fall. When you don't rotate your hips properly or when you fly open, your arm and shoulder have to make up for the mistakes of the body. Pitching's tough enough without adding to the stress.

Here are the basic checkpoints of a proper delivery; follow them carefully and you'll avoid any unnecessary stints on the sidelines:

1—Keep your head over your pivot foot throughout the entire delivery.

2—Don't start any forward momentum toward home plate until your lift leg reaches its apex.

3—Lift—don't kick—your leg up to its maximum height.

4—Hold your hands at the center of gravity—from belly button to upper-chest level.

5—Maintain the same upper-body posture you achieve in the balance phase of the delivery.

6—Always adhere to "tall and fall" (taking a controlled fall toward home plate in the tall posture you achieved at balance) instead of "dip and drive" (pushing off the rubber as you reach your balance, dipping down, and then releasing the baseball).

7—As you begin to move toward home plate, make sure your entire front side—foot, hip, elbow, knee, and glove—is aligned with home plate. This

is what is known as a closed, compact delivery. Hips must stay directional (toward home plate) until the landing leg hits; all hip rotation takes place after this point.

8—*Land with your front side directional but your landing foot "closed off"—a right-hander's left big toe should point slightly toward the third-base side of home plate; a left-hander's right big toe should point slightly toward the first-base side of home plate—blocking off your forward movement. This transfers your forward momentum up through the body and into the arm at your release point, and ultimately ensures a less stressful deceleration of the arm.*

Nolan Ryan is living proof that sound mechanics breed success and longevity. His personal style is remarkably similar to the ideal set of mechanics outlined in this chapter. But it hasn't been easy—Nolan spent a lot of time fine-tuning his delivery in the early, transitional stages of his career.

Tom Seaver was the first person to really get me thinking about the importance of mechanics. We'd talk an awful lot about the link between mechanical efficiency and effectiveness on the mound. He impressed upon me how the purpose of a delivery is to maximize your ability to throw a baseball and generate as much force behind the ball as possible.

After I was traded to the Angels, Tom Morgan, my new pitching coach, stepped in to play a major role in my development.

I had a tendency to fly open like a swinging door (open up my front side too early). Tom identified the problem and had an unusual method of solving it: He would stand at the exact spot where my landing leg hit at the end of the delivery. I couldn't open up without hitting him—he basically functioned as a block or barricade, a very effective way to force me to stay closed.

Jeff Torborg, my catcher with the Angels, also kept a watchful eye on my mechanics. He could tell when I stayed closed and compact, or whether I was drifting. He'd walk out to the mound and remind me of what I was doing right or wrong. Torborg is a very astute baseball man.

Alan Ashby, formerly of the Houston Astros, probably caught me longer than anyone else. Alan recognized when I opened up too soon or rushed my delivery. He understood pitch selection, how I liked to throw to particular hitters, and he could anticipate what to call. We were always on the same wavelength.

Les Moss, my pitching coach with the Astros, had the intuitive understanding of a Tom Seaver. Les always knew when his pitchers were struggling with their mechanics, and he had all sorts of drills for curing mechanical woes. Les would stand on the back of the mound, watching carefully to ensure that my motion wasn't rushed. And if you had trouble with your curveball, he would have you shorten up on your delivery while throwing on the backside of the mound. He'd have us throw, in effect, uphill off the back of the mound to rehearse the proper upper body and arm alignment needed to get a curveball to break in a downward direction.

Tom House is another advocate of sound mechanics. When I first joined the Rangers he mentioned his four absolutes of pitching: balance, direction, deception/launch, and weight transfer. Well, to be honest, this terminology was something I had to evaluate for a while. We were speaking two completely different languages.

Once I finally figured out what Tom was talking about, I realized we were in 100 percent agreement. The four absolutes do, in fact, go hand in hand with throwing a baseball properly. I've stayed in line with the four absolutes throughout my career, though I never put a name on them. I was intuitively doing the right things by just allowing my body to dictate what felt comfortable. And, of course, hitters have a knack for telling you when your mechanics are out of synch.

Every pitcher has the potential for sound mechanics. But first you must establish checkpoints aligned in proper secquence: a string of key elements in a delivery repeated identically every time you pitch. If all your checkpoints are executed to perfection, then you shouldn't have any problems with drifting, rushing, or other mechanical flaws.

In my delivery, for instance, I have to bring the knee of my lift leg up to shoulder level before I start any movement toward home plate. This is my most important checkpoint. Any movement in the direction of the plate before I've finished lifting my leg will destroy my sense of balance—the first absolute. In this initial phase, my hands are parallel to my chest and my stance is closed to maximize deception.

When my knee reaches its full height, I position my body as tall as possible, break my hands, come out with my left side closed, and take a controlled fall and drive movement until my landing leg hits. Head and shoulders always take a route toward the plate, not off in the direction of first or third base. Hips also should be on a parallel line with the plate, though it isn't easy. We'll get into that later on.

Tom House teaches this tall-and-fall approach to the young Rangers pitchers. It's the opposite of the old dip-and-drive method—you would drive or push off the rubber to gain momentum. Tom Seaver was a dip-and-drive type of pitcher. You could see it in Jerry Koosman. And I was somewhat similar to Seaver and Koosman back in the 1960s, but not quite as exaggerated as they were.

The older you get, the harder it is to push off the rubber in dip-and-drive fashion. It requires a lot of physical strength and makes it tough to throw a curveball. The dip and drive flattens you out; your movements are more parallel to the ground. But the taller you are, the better your leverage as you throw in a downward direction. By increasing the angle of my release point,

•

MECHANICS

•

then, it's as if I'm even taller on the mound. Dip and drive gives up some of that advantage. That's why I tell young pitchers to follow the tall-and-fall method of pitching. Tom has worked with my son Reid on the tall-and-fall theory, and he's responded really well.

The second checkpoint in my delivery is that you cannot throw the ball until your landing foot hits the ground. The foot hits the ground and then you deliver the pitch—it's as simple as that.

In this deception/launch stage of the pitching motion, you want to stay closed as long as possible. A closed delivery allows the hitter less time to see the ball. Certain pitchers, just because of the nature of their delivery and arm position, are tougher to read than others. A hitter struggling to find the release point is out of his comfort zone, thus making the pitcher more effective. And by standing taller on the mound, my release point becomes a lot harder to pick up.

Pitchers who are tall and explode to the plate—rather than drift off in the direction of first or third base—never have problems with weight transfer. You accelerate toward home plate, but the final thrust comes from hip rotation. Everything blends together at the end of the delivery in one smooth rhythm. Your head should be parallel to your landing leg as the throwing arm decelerates after the pitch.

I've always had pretty good mechanics, but nobody is perfect. Tom's company, Bio-Kinetics, Inc., videotaped my delivery while I was pitching for Houston in 1988, and then again with the Rangers in 1989. I studied the computer analysis of the video to figure out what I was doing wrong and how to correct it.

In 1988, for instance, the analysis indicated I was drifting forward before getting my lift leg up to full height. And this drift was forcing me to open up my hips too soon. I certainly don't want to fall into any bad habits.

The stick figures on the computer printout reinforced the importance of my checkpoints—that I can't move toward home plate before getting my lift leg up as high as it will go, and that all my force has to be thrust toward the plate, not off to one side or the other.

Compare my mechanics in '88 to '89 and you'll see a few interesting changes. My higher release point improved the efficiency of my weight transfer—my head stayed more in line with my front knee in the launch position. This refinement reduced the stress placed on my shoulder as my arm decelerated.

The older you get, the harder it is to maintain strength and timing. The number one key, then, is proper mechanics; it will lessen the risk of injury while enhancing the prospect of success.

All pitchers are unique. Guys are born with different builds, talents, mental outlooks, and levels of coordination. But pitchers, regardless of individual style, must learn the same principles of throwing a baseball. Then you have to account for natural ability and plug in that variable. Pitchers are going to maintain their distinct styles, but what they do in their delivery—as far as timing is concerned—should be the same.

Jeff Russell and I are very similar. He has a little bit of a timing dip in his delivery—he brings his upper body and knee close together, almost like a sandwich, as he lifts his leg. This is his checkpoint to ensure he doesn't rush, a rhythm-timing mechanism that puts him in a better position to begin his controlled fall toward home plate. My main checkpoint, of course, is to get my knee up to my shoulder. Two different checkpoints, two different pitchers. But we're still on target. It doesn't matter what checkpoint you have as long as you can still find a way to shoot straight.

Charlie Hough is very efficient; his delivery isn't stressful. And he's throwing the knuckleball, so timing—not force—is

(continued on page 62)

MECHANICS

▲
FASTBALL The fastball is gripped across the seams, with the index and middle fingers comfortably spread. In throwing the fastball, the force is driven *through* the ball.

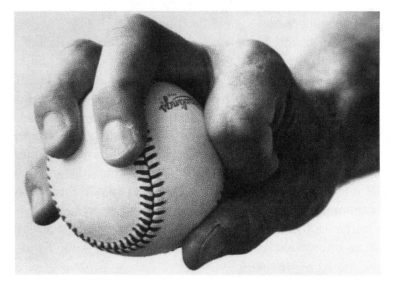

▲
CURVE The curve is gripped with the middle finger along the seam, and the index finger close by it. The downward wrist snap drives the force *across* the ball.

◀
CHANGEUP The "circle change" is gripped with the index finger tucked back against the thumb, and middle and ring fingers along the seams. The ball slides off those fingers, with the primary force driven *alongside* the ball, reducing its speed deceptively.

MECHANICS

crucial. A knuckler won't be effective, in fact, if you try to throw it too hard. Charlie's release point always remains the same. If the release point on a knuckler varies even slightly, then the movement on the ball and your ability to control it will suffer accordingly.

A curveball is like a knuckleball: You won't be effective unless your delivery is consistent. My curveball has improved and developed in direct proportion to my mechanics. As my mechanics got better, I was able to throw the curveball with more consistency and it became a much tougher pitch to hit.

Throwing a curve is based on the idea that as speed increases, pressure decreases. The more seams that spin in the direction of the pitch, the greater the resistance placed on the rotation and the more the pitch will curve. This explains why a lot of young pitchers get into trouble by overthrowing the curveball. You don't have to throw it hard to get it to break; it breaks because of the rotation you put on it by gripping it across the seams.

To throw a curveball, all you have to do is set your forearm, wrist, and fingers in a karate chop–type position and rotate your fingertips over the top of the seams to get the ball to break. Your middle finger is placed next to the seam, the index finger provides support while the thumb is placed underneath to get the most rotation at release point. Your arm speed is the same as when throwing a fastball; the difference is that you're putting rotation over the top of the baseball instead of applying force through the center of the baseball.

High velocity and the curveball don't mix. That's a given. But you can't throw an effective curve unless your elbow is at shoulder height and your shoulder, elbow, and forearm form a 90-degree angle as the arm accelerates. An elbow at shoulder height provides you with adequate leverage to get that rotation over the top of the ball while minimizing the strain on your elbow.

Young pitchers—and even some veteran starters—often struggle with their mechanics when they move from a full windup to the stretch. While the windup helps generate more momentum, there's no real difference between the mechanics of the two motions.

Until you break your hands and start toward home plate, all a windup does is place you in a proper position. Well, pitching out of the stretch simplifies this whole process; it cuts down on the movement needed to launch the baseball. You go directly into your leg lift from a position that starts with your front side already in proper alignment. If there's any difference in your mechanics from balance point on when you pitch out of the stretch, then you're doing something wrong.

My biggest problem with the stretch is holding guys on—a high leg kick affords a base runner the time he needs to get a good jump. I'm forced to break up my rhythm so a base runner can't time me. Perhaps I'll hold the ball a little longer, or throw a pitch without holding the ball as long. Occasionally I'll try my normal leg kick, or I might go with an abbreviated leg kick, just to show a guy like Rickey Henderson a different look.

The high leg kick is a Nolan Ryan trademark. I've always believed that the higher you lift your leg, the more force you'll generate toward home plate and the better your leverage will be. I talked with Tom House about this and asked him to run my theory through the computer. Sure enough, the computer analysis proved that about 4–6 percent more energy is generated when you lift your leg six inches higher. I guess I was right. But I didn't require objective proof to know that a high leg kick was worth the effort; it felt comfortable, so I stuck with it.

Tom and I enjoy discussing mechanics, especially when it concerns my boy Reid. Tom has taught Reid to keep the big toe on the foot of his lift leg pointing down. I'm convinced, though, that toe-up is more mechanically sound for a pitcher. That's

MECHANICS

what I do. I feel it allows you to lift your leg higher.

I've shown Tom photos of my delivery, clearly demonstrating that my toe points upward. Tom conceded that I was correct, that toe-up was better, but only if a pitcher can point the toe up in line with the knee. Reid had a tendency to let his foot drift to the outside of the knee. And Tom taught him toe-down to solve that problem. It was an easier technique to get across.

Proper mechanics is the key to success—I've stressed that to Reid on many occasions. He has a better understanding of that now, and he probably has a better delivery than he's ever had before.

Both of my boys use my delivery as a role model. They feel they're capable of being effective with it, so I don't see any reason to discourage them. I've had my share of success with it, that's for sure.

Physical Conditioning

4

STEP 1: Strength Training

I don't believe in the no-pain, no-gain philosophy of weight training. If you're doing a specific exercise and you experience pain, *stop;* your body is trying to tell you there's a problem.

I'm not talking about the slight discomfort that comes from an overload situation—when you're increasing resistance by lifting more weight or accelerating the intensity of your training by adding more reps and sets, for example. You're going to feel fatigued when that kind of workout is over. And the next day, yeah, you'll be stiff and tight, knowing full well that you did more than your usual routine the day before. But it's not an unpleasant sensation; it's a feeling of satisfaction.

Still, you should be able to go out the next day, warm up gradually, and feel that stiffness and soreness dissipate slowly and surely. Then you know you're on the proper program and not overloading yourself until you reach muscle fatigue, or pushing too hard and driving a muscle to the point where you're going to have some ill effects.

Gene Coleman taught me to stay within my limits of strength while always varying the program enough to make sure it's fresh. Stimulating a muscle requires modifying your daily workout every now and then—keep your body guessing what's coming next.

Gene divided my workout into cycles to prevent me from hitting a training plateau: I might do three sets of leg curls for my hamstrings on the first training day, cut it back to two sets during the next training session, and perform five sets for the workout after that. This cyclical approach ensures that my hamstrings, a muscle group that's given me some problems, won't fatigue as quickly.

My cycles depend on how I'm feeling physically, what our travel schedule dictates, the amount of weight I've been lifting, and whether I'm rested or tired. So I don't have a set plan.

**PHYSICAL
CONDITIONING**

Overall, though, my weight workout hasn't changed much since I hooked up with Gene in 1980. As I mentioned earlier, the Astros train on Nautilus machines. I'd been lifting on Universal equipment with the Angels, so I had to make a few basic adjustments. It was really just a matter of learning the specifics of the Nautilus machines—how to use them properly—and integrating the new movements into my program.

Then Gene decided to include squats (to provide added strength for my legs, a must for a pitcher), bench press (a chest exercise for upper-body strength), and lunges (for the gluteus maximus, a muscle that's put under a lot of stress during the delivery) with a barbell.

Free-weight exercises, performed with either barbells or dumbbells, are better than machines because your body, rather than the machine, is forced to support the weight. Handling and balancing a set of dumbbells or a bar increases muscular coordination. And so your muscles learn to compensate for any increased resistance by growing stronger and more powerful.

Tom House added the military press with a barbell to my program when I joined the Rangers—I used to execute this movement on a machine. The military press builds strength in the front part of the shoulder, an area that undergoes considerable stress when you pitch off a mound. And he also taught me the bent-over dumbbell row, an effective back (latissimus) exercise that improves a pitcher's posture and overall trunk stability.

Rangers pitchers, myself included, follow a balanced strength-training routine. The goal is to compensate in the weight room for the demands of throwing a baseball over the long campaign. Here's Tom House on the value of strength training for a pitcher.

A pitcher has to establish a firm base of muscle strength to handle the wear and tear of pitching a baseball. Muscle strength

is the first line of defense against microtears in the muscle tissue and injuries to tendons and ligaments. If tendons and ligaments give out on you from a lack of muscle strength, then it's bad news for your bones: Bone chips, stress fractures, and structural problems are the likely consequence of tendon and ligament injuries.

Strength training, using resistance weight training to build maximal muscle force, relies on lifting heavy weights for fewer repetitions. The heavy weight lifts that Nolan performs in his strength-training program are his insurance policy against the fatigue-related ailments that force pitchers to the sidelines.

Nolan, an ardent advocate of staying healthy and fit year-round, adheres to both an in-season and off-season strength-training regimen. The weight workout remains exactly the same from one season to the next; the only difference is the volume—specific poundages lifted—per exercise. Nolan trains to muscle failure in the off-season while in-season he'll only lift 70 percent of his max weight; there's no throwing off a mound during the off-season strength program.

Strength-building reaches its peak in the off-season (October to January). I lift my max weight three days a week (Mondays, Wednesdays, and Fridays), while avoiding any skill work—pitching. I just don't want to ask too much out of my arm during the base phase of the conditioning cycle.

Once January rolls around, though, I'll start decreasing the weight by 15 percent and do some pitching on flat ground in anticipation of spring training. By the time I get to Port Charlotte, Florida, I'm ready to pitch off a mound, and the poundage drops to 70 percent of my maximum workload. This maintenance phase continues throughout the season—I lift on the first and third days after pitching.

●

PHYSICAL CONDITIONING

●

69

I also hit the weight room on the day I pitch. I'll go through most of my exercises (though no squats or bench press) for one set with a really light weight. I do this prior to going out on the field to perform my pre-game throwing and stretching. It makes my arm feel loose, kind of like a last-minute tuneup.

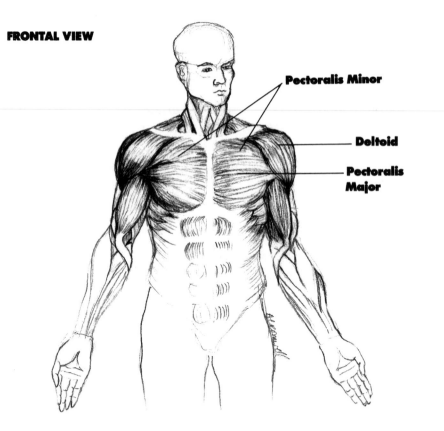

FRONTAL VIEW

Pectoralis Minor

Deltoid

Pectoralis Major

FRONTAL The main muscle groups that accelerate the arm while pitching are pectoralis minor, deltoid, and pectoralis major.

Balancing strength is what my weight program is all about. You have three muscle groups that accelerate the arm and two muscle groups that decelerate the arm, and there has to be a balance of strength between both groups. If your muscle strength gets out of whack, well, you're looking at an injury somewhere down the road.

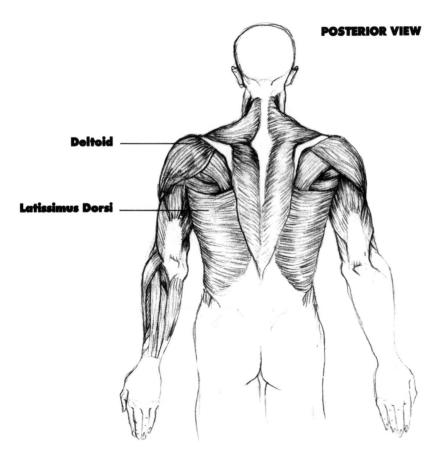

POSTERIOR VIEW

Deltoid

Latissimus Dorsi

POSTERIOR   The main muscle groups that decelerate the arm while pitching are the deltoid and latissimus dorsi.

PHYSICAL CONDITIONING

Usually it's the backside of the arm that's lacking, as there are only two muscle groups to rely on. If you don't allow for this by doing extra work on those backside groups, you'll have a recurrent imbalance. When you decelerate the arm with an imbalance, then you have an overload on those weaker groups. You start getting muscle fatigue, irritated tendons and ligaments, and before you know it you end up with tendinitis or even a muscle tear.

Strength tests for pitchers are designed to identify imbalances before a serious injury occurs. If and when a pitcher lacks strength—say, in the rear shoulder (deltoid) muscle—his weight-training program is altered to make amends. Obviously, poundages are increased to rebuild a weak area.

Pitchers are tested in-season to ensure they're maintaining balanced strength, and in January to monitor the base phase of the strength-building process. And all pitchers must lift specific poundages in a given week, depending on their particular weekly workload; velocity, the number of pitches thrown in a typical week, and mechanical efficiency are all taken into consideration in dictating individual strength requirements.

Tom uses a variation of a standard formula to apply workloads for his pitchers:

$$\frac{1}{2}\ \text{mass} \times \text{velocity}^2 = \text{foot pounds of work}$$

Here is how it's adapted to baseball: You take half of the weight (mass) of a baseball (5 ounces) and multiply that by a pitcher's velocity (squared) as measured by the speed gun. Then you multiply the product of that equation by .01044 (the $\times$ factor, representing the ratio of acceleration and deceleration of the arm), the average number of pitches thrown in a week, and the reciprocal of mechanical efficiency. Since my mechanical efficiency is rated at 93 percent, the reciprocal would be

$$\frac{1}{.93} \text{ or } 1.075.$$

Let's say your weekly workload is 100 pitches thrown at 90 mph with 100 percent mechanical efficiency. That would put about 14,100-foot pounds of stress on the arm. Foot-pounds are a measure of work. The 14,100 figure is easily derived through a standard exercise physiology measurement—in simplified form it looks like this: a weight traveling at x velocity requires y amount of work. In this case, a 5-ounce baseball thrown at 90 mph weighs about 47 pounds. Multiply 47 by the weekly number of pitches (100) and workout days (3) and you end up with 14,100 pounds. The 14,100-pound load, then, becomes that pitcher's maintenance level. He must lift 14,100 pounds in the weight room—per week—to compensate for the loss of strength.

Computer analysis can precisely calculate your level of mechanical efficiency. As a reasonable guideline, you can use the number below that applies to your particular situation:

High school pitchers 80 percent
College pitchers 85 percent
Professional pitchers 85–95 percent

Once a throwing workload is established, Tom adds in another 10,000 pounds to account for the fact that throwing off a mound is a tearing-down process. Thus, for that pitcher with perfect mechanics, his base level of lifting in the off-season would be 24,100 pounds. The last thing a pitcher needs is a strength-deficit situation, especially after he's worked so hard to stay out of trouble.

Tom and I like to work out together in the morning. I'm a real believer in morning workouts. We'll meet in the weight room at Arlington Stadium and talk about exercise techniques, baseball, pitching strategies—it's our 90 minutes to discuss what we want without other people coming in and demanding my time or his time. We look forward to it; it's a ritual we really enjoy.

Training on road trips is a pleasant diversion. What we try to do—since we work out in the morning and hotels aren't usually convenient to the ballpark—is lift at a facility somewhere in town, generally a YMCA, private club, or neighborhood gym. (Oakland is an exception. The A's have a very good weight room, and we'll just go in early and work out before their guys arrive. That makes sense because the hotel in Oakland doesn't have a weight-training facility, so there's no convenient alternative to the Oakland Coliseum.)

I don't mind putting in the hours for training when I'm on the road. During a home stand, however, hanging out at the ballpark from morning until midnight becomes a real disadvantage. There are more demands on my time in Texas. And, of course, I want to see my family as much as possible.

But my workout days are extremely important—well worth the sacrifices I need to make to stay on line with the program.

THE STRENGTH-TRAINING REGIMEN

EXERCISE	SETS	REPS
Squat	3	12-12-12
Lunge	3	12-12-12
Step up	3	12-12-12
Leg extension	3	12-12-12
Leg curl	3	12-12-12
Toe raise	3	12-12-12
Bench press	3	12-12-12
Double chest	3	12-12-12
Arm cross	3	12-12-12
Decline pass	3	12-12-12
Machine row	3	12-12-12
Lat pull	3	12-12-12
Bent-over row	3	12-12-12
Military press	3	12-12-12
Dumbbell curl	3	12-12-12
Standing triceps press	3	12-12-12

NOTE: Don't try to lift a weight you can't handle. The amount of resistance should allow you to execute the movement with perfect form for 12 reps.

PHYSICAL
CONDITIONING

SQUAT
(works quadriceps—thigh—muscle group)

Step under a barbell that's positioned on a rack and let
it rest across the back of your shoulders and trapezius.
Holding on to the bar to balance it, raise it off the rack
as you step back into the starting position (Ill.1). With
your feet positioned slightly wider than hip width and

1

your gaze directed upward, bend your knees and descend until your thighs are parallel to the ground. Your knees should point directly over—not beyond—your toes (Ill. 2). Now dig your heels in, contract your abdominal muscles, and push back up to the starting position.

2

3

LUNGE

(works gluteus maximus)

Holding a barbell across the back of your shoulders, stand upright with your feet together. Keeping your head up, your back straight and your chest out, take a step forward, bending your lead knee and lowering your rear knee almost to the floor (Ill. 3). The step should extend far enough so that your back leg is almost straight. Now push yourself up to the starting position, so that your feet are together. Repeat with the other leg.

STEP UP

(works quadriceps, hamstrings, and hip flexors)

Step up with your left leg onto a flat bench. Then step up with your right leg. Step down with your left leg first, then with the right leg. Repeat, starting with the right leg. Inhale on the way up; exhale on the way down.

LEG EXTENSION
(works quadriceps)

Sit on the seat of a leg-extension machine, hooking your feet under the pads. Extend your legs as far as possible (Ill. 4), flex your thighs, and slowly lower the weight just short of the starting position. Don't let it drop; you need to keep continual pressure on the quads. (*Note:* In order to minimize the chances of recurring chondromalacia patella, I do this exercise so that extension occurs only through the last 15 degrees of extension.)

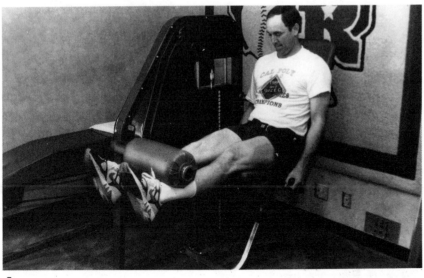

4

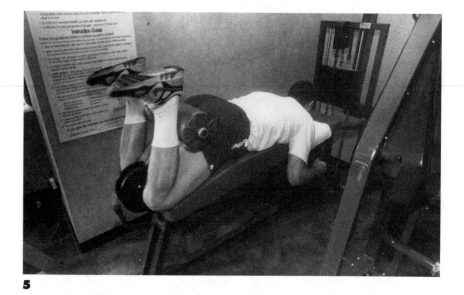

5

LEG CURL

(works hamstrings)

Lie facedown with your heels locked under the pads of the lever mechanism. Flex your feet so that your toes are pointing toward you. Contract your glutes, then curl your legs up as far as possible (Ill. 5). Don't bounce or raise your butt too high off the bench. Then lower the weight slowly to the starting position.

6   TOE RAISE

(works calf—gastrocnemius and soleus—muscles)

Stand with only the balls of your feet on the block of a standing calf raise machine; your heels should extend unsupported beyond the block. (My variation: Do one set with toes straight ahead, one set with toes pointing inward, one set with toes pointing outward.) Slide your shoulders under the pads and straighten your legs. Now lower your heels as far as possible toward the floor—they must extend at least below the level of the block you're standing on. Your body should move as one unit, propelled by your feet. After you come down for a full stretch, rise up as high as possible for a full contraction (Ill. 6).

PHYSICAL CONDITIONING

7

8

BENCH PRESS

(works chest—pectoral—muscles)

Lie on a flat bench with your feet spaced about shoulder-width apart on the floor. Take a medium overhand grip on the bar. Lift the bar off the rack and hold it over your chest at arm's length above you (Ill. 7). Lower the bar slowly until it touches your upper chest; be sure to keep your elbows underneath the bar (don't bring them forward) and don't rotate your upper arm (Ill. 8). Then press the bar back up until your arms are almost locked (Ill. 9).

9

DOUBLE CHEST

Here are the two exercises performed at this station. Arm cross works the overall chest; decline press concentrates on lower chest.

ARM CROSS
(works chest—pectoral—muscles)

10

Adjust the seat to align your shoulders directly above the axis of the movement arms— the axis is marked with red dots. Sit in the seat and fasten the seat belt. Place your legs on the leg rest and relax your lower body. Place your forearms behind and firmly against the movement arm pads. Grasp the handles lightly; thumbs should be underneath the rungs with your upper arms roughly horizontal to the floor. Push with your forearm—try to touch your elbows in front of your chest (Ill. 10). Keep your neck back, chin down, chest up, shoulders down, and back arched. Pause in the forward position. Then lower the weight slowly to a comfortable stretch and repeat.

DECLINE PRESS
(works chest—pectoral—muscles)

Stay seated in the double-chest machine, with the seat at the same height you used for the arm-cross exercise. Place your feet on the foot pad and push to bring the handles forward. Grasp the handles lightly, applying pressure with the palms. Remove your feet from the foot pad, thus enabling the weight to be placed on your hands. Allow the handles to push your arms back in a comfortable stretch. Push forward until your elbows are extended (Ill. 11). Keep your elbows slightly out, your neck and head back, chin down, back arched, chest up, and shoulders down. Lower the weight stack to the starting position and repeat. Exit this machine by depressing the foot pads. Remove the weight from your arms.

11

12

13

MACHINE ROW

(works back—latissimus—and shoulders—deltoids)

Place the movement arm in the rowing position. Unload weight before changing the movement arm. Straddle the seat and from a standing position, lean forward and grasp the lower set of handles with your palms facing each other. Sit on the seat and allow your arms to stretch forward. Then pull back; your arms should be at a slight decline so that when you pull back, your hands are just below your armpits. Adjust the seat if necessary, or use the handles to the sides of your chest by bending your arms. Do not lean back. Keep your elbows back. Pause, lower resistance slowly and smoothly to the stretch position, and repeat. Use a thumbs-up position for the lower handles (Ill. 12) and a thumbs-down position for the upper handles (Ill. 13); the latter provide more resistance.

LAT PULL

(works upper back)

Sit down at a pull-down machine and grasp the bar with a wide grip. Pull the bar down behind your head until it touches your neck (Ill. 14). When doing this movement to the front of the body, sit on a bench, place your feet on the machine, assume a close grip, and pull the bar down until it reaches your chest (Ill. 15).

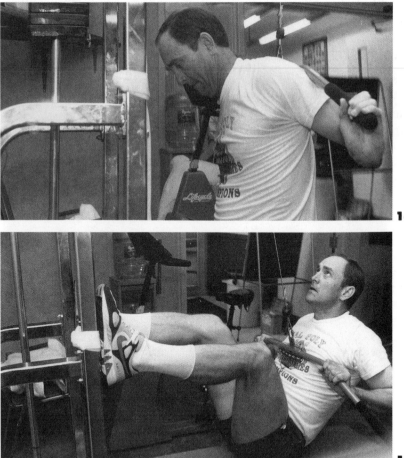

14

15

BENT-OVER ROW

(works upper back)

Grasp a dumbbell in your right hand, and put your left leg and left hand on a bench, your right foot positioned firmly on the floor. Hold the dumbbell at arm's length. Lift the weight up as high as you can (Ill. 16), and lower it slowly, feeling the stretch in your lat muscles. Repeat for the other side, switching foot position accordingly.

16

MILITARY PRESS

(works shoulders)

From a standing position, grip a barbell, keeping your hands shoulder-width apart. Bring the barbell up to shoulder level in front of you, tucking your elbows under as much as possible. Raise the weight over your head (Ill. 17). Hold at the top, then lower the weight to the starting position and repeat.

17

DUMBBELL CURL

(works biceps)

Sit at the edge of a flat bench. Grasp a dumbbell in one hand—palm facing forward, rotate your wrist outward and curl the weight up until it's four inches below your collarbone (Ill. 18). Don't lean back while lifting the weight. Slowly lower the weight and repeat the movement with the other arm.

18

STANDING TRICEPS PRESS
(works triceps)

Because of my previous elbow surgery, I don't like to completely extend the elbow against resistance. Thus, I stand at a pull-down station, grasp the bar, and perform a standing triceps press (Ill. 19). In essence, I block the range of motion to minimize pressure on the elbow in the starting position.

19

STEP 2: Endurance Training

PART 1: LIGHT-DUMBBELL PROGRAM

A solid foundation of endurance will contribute to a pitcher's longevity. All those innings sure place a lot of wear and tear on the arm. So you have to do something to prevent stress-related injuries. You can't just sit back and hope you won't get hurt. And that's where the light-dumbbell program comes into play.

I started doing the Jobe exercises in 1980. The doctors who devised the program understood the importance of concentrating on critical areas in the shoulder—the rotator cuff and supraspinatus—for the health and well-being of a pitcher's arm. I view the light dumbbells as a maintenance device, the best way I know of to sustain muscle and connective-tissue endurance while helping prevent disabling injuries.

I like to perform the light-dumbbell exercises on the same day I do my heavy lifting. During the season, that means the first and third days after pitching; in the off-season, however, it means Mondays, Wednesdays, and Fridays—my standard workout days.

●

PHYSICAL CONDITIONING

●

Tom House is also a firm believer in the value of endurance training. Here's his view.

Endurance training, stimulating the ability of a muscle to produce force continually over a period of time, allows a pitcher to perform at the top of his game throughout what can seem like an endless summer. Muscle endurance is the ability of a muscle to fire up at maximum efficiency, not just three times, but 300 times.

Just look at the awesome endurance requirements of pitching: A starter often logs more than 200 innings a year—if he's effective—and a reliable reliever has to bounce back quickly from outing to outing. Kenny Rogers, a left-handed reliever on the Rangers, might hurl two innings and strike out five batters one night and be asked to retire a key hitter or two the next. Well, Kenny isn't just doing this for an isolated series of games in April; he's required to answer the call from April through October.

Kenny's only defense against muscle fatigue is a comprehensive endurance-training regimen, and that means using the elastic-cord and light-dumbbell program for pitchers. But, as Nolan points out, the need for muscle endurance is a fairly recent discovery.

Before the late 1970s, a pitcher was pretty much on his own for building endurance. Little was known about the rotator cuff and its significance to pitchers. As sports medicine evolved, training techniques like the light-dumbbell exercises cropped up to minimize the incidence of arm problems. Here's an illustration of how things have changed.

I developed bone chips in my elbow in 1975, an ailment I attribute to throwing a lot of curveballs under the stress of im-

proper mechanics. My arm was simply not in the correct position to throw the pitch. I remember asking the doctor who performed the surgery on my elbow if he had a specific rehab program. He told me there was no rehab; I'd know when I could start throwing again based on how my arm felt. That was the extent of the recommended rehab. Now if I had bone chips in my elbow in 1990—like Jeff Russell—I'd be placed on a strict rehab regimen as soon after the operation as possible.

A pitcher often has to trust his own judgment in dealing with a serious injury. I pitched through the entire 1986 season with a tear in the tendon of my elbow. Certain orthopedists said surgery was the only method of correcting the problem. At my age, though, I believed in giving the elbow an opportunity to heal on its own.

I went home after the season ended and just took it easy. Around the middle of December my elbow finally stopped hurting. After another 30 days of inactivity I was able to pitch again. Obviously, I was right; the injury did heal with rest.

Unfortunately, there's still some scar tissue in the elbow, just enough to prevent me from using the elastic-cord program. The light dumbbells are my principal source of muscle endurance.

THE LIGHT-DUMBBELL REGIMEN

Perform three sets of 10 repetitions for each exercise.

RAINBOW

Stand erect. Hold a dumbbell in each hand at waist level (Ill. 20), palms away from the body. Slowly bend your elbows and pull the back of each hand to your chin, keeping palms down (Ill. 21). Continue to pull the weights past your chin until each arm is extended straight over your head (palms in). Then rotate palms out (Ill. 22), keep arms straight, and slowly lower weights to the starting (palms down) position. Turn your palms out and repeat.

20

21

22

SHOULDER ABDUCTION/ADDUCTION

Stand erect with your hands at your sides, palms facing the body. Hold a dumbbell in each hand. Keep your elbows straight, and slowly raise your arms (abduction) straight out to your sides (Ill. 23). Stop the motion when both arms are over your head, palms facing out. Slowly lower your arms to the starting position (adduction) and repeat.

23

SUPRASPINATUS

Hold a dumbbell in each hand, thumbs down, arms at your sides. Slowly lift your arms straight out to your sides until they reach shoulder height (Ill. 24). Raise your arms in a plane about 30 degrees forward to vertical. Do not raise arms higher than shoulder level. Slowly lower your arms to the starting position and repeat.

24

PHYSICAL CONDITIONING

EXTERNAL ROTATION

Lie on your right side with your left elbow close against the ribs. Hold a dumbbell in your left hand (Ill. 25). Slowly raise the weight until your knuckles are pointing toward the ceiling (Ill. 26). Slowly lower the dumbbell to the starting position and repeat. Repeat with the right arm.

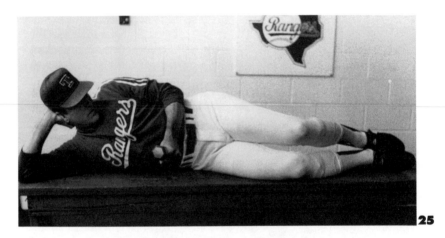

25

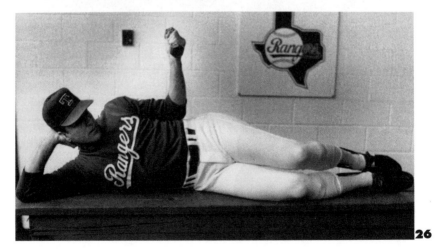

26

BUTTERFLY

Hold a dumbbell in each hand. Lie with your back on a bench or table, palms facing inward, elbows slightly bent and arms held straight over your shoulders. Slowly lower the weights to your sides (Ill. 27). Keep a slight bend in your elbows. Return to the starting position and repeat.

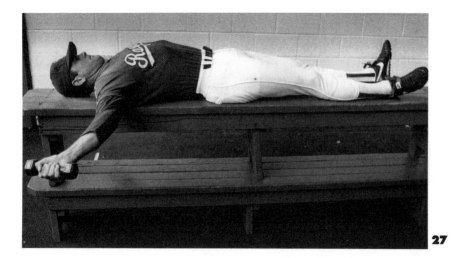

27

UPWARD ROTATION

Hold a dumbbell in each hand. Lie with your stomach on a bench, arms raised to shoulder level, elbows at right angles and weights pointed toward the floor (Ill. 28). Slowly lift the dumbbells upward until forearms are parallel to the floor (Ill. 29). Return to starting position and repeat.

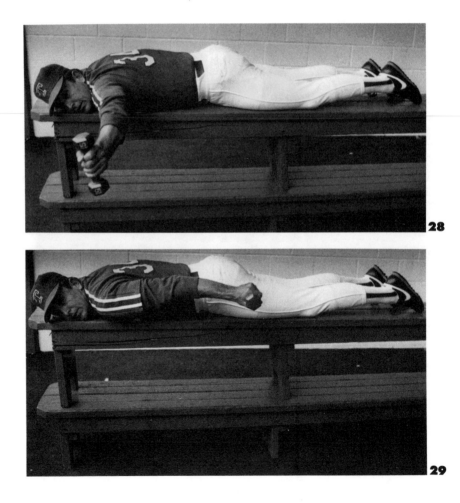

28

29

PULL-OVER

Hold a dumbbell in each hand. Lie with your back on a bench, shoulders flexed overhead and level with the floor, elbows flexed 90 degrees and palms in-ward (Ill. 30). Keep your elbows flexed and pull your arms forward until they're parallel with your sides. Return to starting position and repeat.

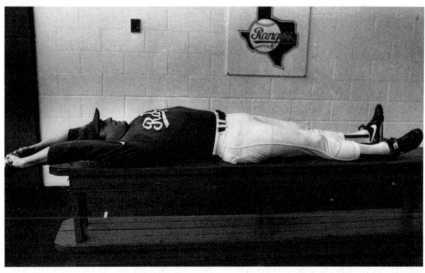

30

PART 2: THE ELASTIC-CORD PROGRAM

Most pitchers can also enhance endurance through proper application of the elastic cord. Here's Tom House to tell you more about it.

A physical-conditioning program for pitchers is geared to striking a balance between muscle strength and endurance, tendon/ligament strength and flexibility, and optimal cartilage and bone density. A pitcher doesn't have to be strong to throw his hardest in the short run, but he must be muscle-strong and muscle-durable to throw his hardest over a succession of starts or relief appearances during a 162-game major-league season.

The elastic cord, a piece of tubing with a baseball on one end and a strap that attaches to a fence on the other, builds a base of muscle endurance and adds to tendon and ligament strength. Believe me, it's nothing new. I used to cut up inner tubes and experiment with all sorts of exercises. It was a crude yet effective endurance-training device.

I think the Kansas City Royals did the initial studies on surgical tubing way back in the dark ages of the early 1970s. These tests failed to yield the missing piece of the puzzle: What degree of resistance does a cord ask out of an arm as it goes through the range-of-motion exercises?

An important question. Back when I pitched for the Atlanta Braves, I took the tubing with me on the road. But I had no idea how many sets and reps to do, and I couldn't gauge—objectively—what kind of workout I was getting.

The technicians at Spri Products, an exercise-equipment company based in Chicago, took the guesswork out of elastic-resistance exercise. They used a Cybex isokinetic machine to determine the exact tensile strength, resistance, and foot-pounds of stress placed on an arm as it stretches the cord to its varying lengths.

CYBEX TUBING TENSILE-STRENGTH STUDY

A 12-inch piece of tubing attached to a fence strap was used for this test.

GREEN (light resistance)		
ORIGINAL LENGTH	**(EQUALS)**	**FOOT-POUNDS OF TORQUE**
×2	(24 in.)	11.5
×3	(36 in.)	18.0
×4	(48 in.)	23.0
×5	(60 in.)	52.0
RED (medium resistance)		
×2	(24 in.)	12.5
×3	(36 in.)	14.0
×4	(48 in.)	18.0
×5	(60 in.)	61.5
BLUE (heavy resistance)		
×2	(24 in.)	19.0
×3	(36 in.)	27.0
×4	(48 in.)	48.0
×5	(60 in.)	72.0

SOURCE: Spri Products.

PHYSICAL CONDITIONING

Each pitcher on the Rangers staff has a different way of integrating the cord into his conditioning program. Kenny Rogers is a good case study.

Kenny does very little heavy weight training with dumbbells; instead, he concentrates on performing 10 times the standard volume of exercise on the blue—or heaviest—cord. As a relief pitcher, Kenny requires endurance more than absolute strength. If he was going to enter the starting rotation—a distinct possibility for the '91 season—he'd have to change his routine to include more muscle-strength building in the weight room.

Rangers pitchers rely on the cord year-round; however, as with the heavier weights, they'll use the cord at max resistance in the off-season and only at 70 percent of max resistance in-season. Frequency of the program will vary depending on a pitcher's throwing workload, fatigue level, and other pertinent variables.

The cord is a great warm-up to a weight workout. It is, however, a warm-up that pays real muscle-endurance dividends. Perform the six recommended exercises for three sets of 10 reps. Start with the light (green) cord and work your way up to heavier resistance. If you're traveling and don't have access to a gym, you can use the tubing in lieu of weight training.

The beauty of the elastic-cord program—and this is also true for the light dumbbells—is that the exercises directly imitate the throwing motions of a pitcher. By rehearsing the motion with a cord or weight, then, your endurance will be increased when you release the ball during the delivery of a pitch.

THE ELASTIC-CORD REGIMEN

Perform all exercises for three sets of 10 repetitions each.

EXTERNAL SHOULDER ROTATION

Positioning: Attach the unilateral (one-arm) tube to a fence at waist height and assume a square, bent-knee stance. The shoulder not being worked should face the fence. Position the exercise shoulder out in front of the body in loose pack position, i.e., 50-degree angle of shoulder abduction—movement of a limb away from the middle of the body—and 30 degrees of horizontal shoulder flexion—bending in contrast to extending.

Execution: Externally rotate the shoulder, extend and straighten the arm, flex the wrist, and hold for two seconds (Ill. 31). Return on a horizontal plane with a straight arm to the starting position and repeat.

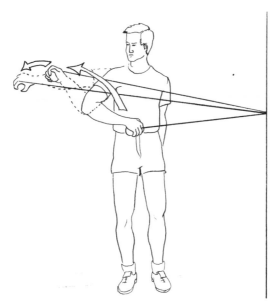

31

INTERNAL SHOULDER ROTATION

Positioning: Attach the tube to a fence at shoulder height and assume a square, bent-knee stance. Exercise shoulder faces the fence; shoulder position is the same as in external shoulder rotation.

Execution: Internally rotate the shoulder, then push across the body, palm facing forward, and hold the extended position for two seconds (Ill. 32). Then slowly return on a horizontal plane to the starting position.

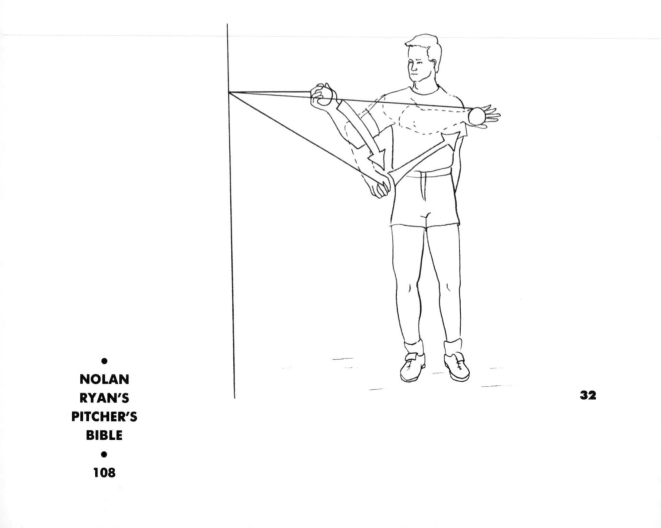

SIDE SHOULDER RAISE

Positioning: Attach the tube to a fence at ankle height and assume a square, bent-knee stance. The shoulder not being worked should face the fence. Bend your elbow and position the thumb on top of the hipbone with thumb pointing at belly button.

Execution: Raise your arm up and away from the side, with the hands slightly higher than the elbow. Once the elbow has reached shoulder height, then externally rotate the shoulder and face the palm and forearm toward the sky (Ill. 33). Then return to the starting position.

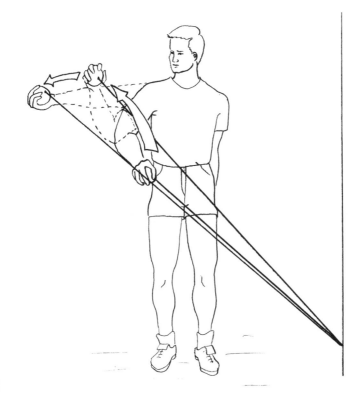

33

SIDE SHOULDER PULLDOWN

Positioning: Attach the tube to a fence above head height (kneel if the fence is not high enough) and face exercise shoulder toward the fence. Assume a staggered lunge stance, with the opposite side foot out slightly in front of the exercise arm.

Execution: Pull the arm down in front of the body while internally rotating the shoulder toward the opposite side of the body (Ill. 34). Then raise the hand to shoulder height, pause for two seconds, and return on a horizontal plane to the starting position.

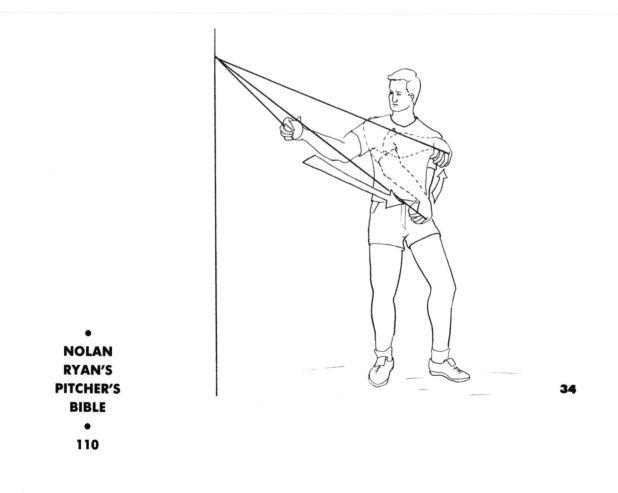

34

SHOULDER EXTENSION/
ELBOW EXTENSION

Positioning: Attach the tube to a fence at shoulder height and face the fence. Bend your elbow and form a 90-degree angle with upper and lower arm. Assume a staggered lunge stance, with the opposite side leg slightly out in front of your body.

Execution: Pull your bent arm down and back behind the body, straighten the elbow, flex the wrist, and pause for two seconds (Ill. 35). Return slowly by coming back around the body, keeping your hand slightly lower than the shoulder.

35

ELBOW FLEXION/SHOULDER FLEXION

Positioning: Attach the tube to a fence at ankle height and face exercise shoulder away from the fence at a 45-degree angle. Begin with the exercise arm straight and away from the side of your body. Assume a slightly staggered lunge stance.

Execution: Hold your elbow behind the body, bend the elbow, bring the palm of the hand to the armpit. Then extend and straighten the arm and push it across the body in line with the opposite shoulder (Ill. 36). After holding for three seconds, return slowly to the starting position.

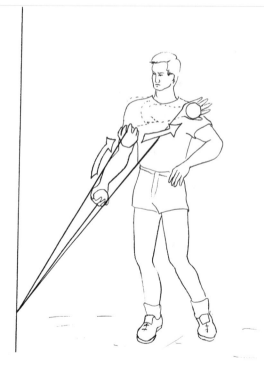

STEP 3: Flexibility, Aerobics, and Abdominal Program

All pitchers can improve the flexibility and elasticity of their muscles. Genetics, naturally, will dictate the limits of your flexibility. That's a fact. But the more flexible you are, the less likely it is you'll be injured and the better your chances of maximizing your ability.

Strength and flexibility through range of motion allows for a more efficient application of power. In practical terms, flexible muscles make it a lot easier to put added power on the pitch; you're able to progress from balance to launch to weight transfer smoothly and in a good rhythm.

I started stretching to improve my flexiblity in high school. Our baseball team got together before the game and did side-straddle hops and the hurdler's stretch. The old classics. In those days everybody thought you bounced when you stretched.

Bob Anderson, who worked for the Angels in the 1970s, was the first person who'd done any practical research on stretching—it was his area of expertise. I spent many hours trying all his stretches. I honestly believed his input would be beneficial to my career.

Bob stressed that distance-running and stretching were of great value to pitchers. He had a lot of good ideas, but limited exposure to baseball. Athletes must gear their physical training to the particular requirements of their sport, so I modified Bob's program to suit my needs.

Gene Coleman helped me pick and choose from Anderson's stretches. Gene and I talked about the proper approach to stretching for pitchers, and between the two of us, we developed a program addressing a pitcher's flexibility requirements.

Each pitcher's stretching plan depends on his particular physical strengths and weaknesses. Since I suffer from lower-back trouble, my stretching concentrates on warming up that area. I also focus on the hamstrings, another part of my body that's taken a beating from the strain of being a power pitcher.

Years ago, while pitching for the Astros one night in Shea Stadium, I came down hard on my landing leg and the hamstring just popped. I could hardly walk. I flew home to Texas and checked in with a doctor. He pretty much turned my rehab over to Gene.

Gene sought out the track coach at the University of Texas, an old friend of his, for some hamstring advice. The coach recommended running in the deep end of a pool, so I combined underwater distance-running and interval sprints in a daily workout in my pool in Alvin. I did this routine 10 days in a row. On the tenth day I went out and ran a mile and a quarter on hard ground—and that was with a severe hamstring pull—without any discomfort.

So I started running in the pool on a regular basis. It was a more interesting alternative to the monotony of sitting on a stationary bike, and spared my ankles and hamstrings the pounding of running on the road.

My pool in Arlington isn't heated—it doesn't heat up from the sun until late afternoon when I'm already at the ballpark—so I don't run in the water as often as I did in Houston. I may do it twice a week; it breaks up my routine so my body won't hit a training plateau or get bored.

I ride the stationary bike for 30 to 45 minutes on the first three days after I pitch. Then I'll sprint on the outfield grass for another 20 minutes—assuming my hamstrings can take it.

During the off-season, I'll ride the stationary bike Mondays, Wednesdays, and Fridays (Ill. 37). And if my hamstring pain isn't too severe, I'll run for 45 minutes on the country roads near my ranch in Alvin. I wait until most people go to work at 9:00 A.M. so there's no one around. I might see two cars the whole time—it's really nice.

37

I'm a believer in a balanced aerobic program. An integrated package of activities helps me stay strong in the late innings of a ball game. Again, Tom has a thing or two to add.

Pitchers need stamina—the cardiovascular and respiratory efficiency required to pump blood, oxygen, and nutrients throughout the system. Stamina accelerates the body's natural healing process; a pitcher is always healing the wounds (microtears and muscle strains) incurred by throwing a baseball off an elevated mound.

You can't develop stamina without aerobic exercise—pushing the heart and breathing rate up for 25–40 minutes, three days a week. Nolan does more aerobic training than most pitchers, but that's consistent with his overall work ethic; Tex is quite simply the best-conditioned athlete I've ever met.

Training the midsection is another basic component of a pitcher's conditioning program. I think it's very simple—you generate force with your legs and apply it through your arms, but the energy is transferred through the midsection. It's a three-link chain and you're only as strong as the weakest link. Poorly developed abs, then, can actually lead to arm problems down the line. And strong abdominals reduce the pressure on your lower-back muscles. My lower-back problems constantly remind me that I'd be even worse off if I wasn't performing a steady diet of sit-ups and stretching.

I work my abs the first three days after a start in-season; during the off-season I'll train the midsection on Mondays, Wednesdays, and Fridays.

THE ABDOMINAL REGIMEN

SIT-UPS

(knees bent and feet flat on the ground)

Perform one set, 10 reps of each exercise. Do this program on the first three days after pitching during the season and three days per week in the off-season.

1. Curl up by bringing rib cage toward your pelvis with hands behind head (Ill. 38).

2. V-up: Elbows and knees come up at the same time (Ill. 39).

3. Reach between knees: Reach between knees with both hands.

4. Reach outside knees: Reach outside bent knees.

5. Alternate in and outside knees.

6. Crunch up: Bring rib cage toward pelvis and pause for a count of eight; do eight reps.

7. Cross right knee and curl up: right elbow to right knee with right knee crossed over left.

8. Cross right knee and twist up: Twist and touch left elbow to right knee with right knee crossed over left.

9. Cross right knee and alternate curl up and twist up.

10. Cross left knee and curl up: left elbow to left knee with left knee crossed over right.

38

39

11. Cross left knee and twist up: Twist and touch right elbow to left knee with left knee crossed over right.

12. Cross left knee and alternate curl up and twist up.

13. Bring right knee up and curl up: Keep left knee bent and foot on the ground, curl up and bring right knee to right elbow.

14. Bring left knee up and curl up: Keep right knee bent and foot on the ground, curl up and bring left knee to left elbow.

15. Bring right knee up and twist up: Keep left knee bent and foot on the ground, twist up and bring right knee to left elbow.

16. Bring left knee up and twist up: Keep right knee bent and foot on the ground, twist up and bring left knee to right elbow.

17. Straighten right leg and curl up: Start with both knees bent, bring right leg up with knee straight, curl up and bring right elbow to right knee.

18. Straighten left leg and curl up: Start with both knees bent, bring left leg up with knee straight, curl up and bring left elbow to left knee.

19. Straighten/bent right leg: On alternate reps bring right knee to right elbow in straight-leg and bent-leg positions.

20. Straighten/bent left leg: On alternate reps bring left knee to left elbow in straight-leg and bent-leg positions.

21. Straighten left leg and twist up: Bring left leg up with knee straight, twist up and bring right elbow to left knee.

22. Straighten right leg and twist up: Bring right leg up with knee straight, twist up and bring left elbow to right knee.

23. Cross ankles and alternate reaching up: Extend both legs straight up and touch right hand to left foot and vice versa.

40

24. Pump sit-up: Alternate touching opposite elbow to opposite knee, extending the other leg (Ill. 40).

25. Reach side to side: Curl up with hands at sides, bend, and touch right hand to right leg. Relax and repeat on left side.

26. Drop extended legs side to side: Extend both legs straight up, slowly lower them to the right until they're six inches off the ground. Relax and repeat on left side.

27. Knee drop: Cross legs at ankles, knees bent, drop both knees to the left and then to the right.

28. Seal: From push-up position, raise chest and shoulders off the ground while keeping waist on the ground. Slowly turn to right and left to stretch abdominal muscles (Ill. 41).

41

You have to prepare your body for the activity of pitching. Before I pick up a ball I want to stretch, do my running, get my heart rate up, and make sure I'm loose. During the season I stretch every day to stay loose; in the off-season I'll stretch just prior to lifting weights (Mondays, Wednesdays, and Fridays). You can blow a ball game by going out to pitch in the first inning without warming up properly. That's not fair to your teammates—or yourself.

●

PHYSICAL CONDITIONING

●

THE PRE-GAME WARM-UP AND FLEXIBILITY REGIMEN

WARM-UP INTERVAL (RUNNING AND STRETCHING)
Jog 200–300 yards.

SIDE-STEP HAMSTRING

Assume a squat position with your weight resting on the flexed right knee, foot flat on the ground, and the left leg extended sideways, toe-up. Hold for six seconds. Raise and lower your left foot and hold for three seconds. After the third interval, grasp right ankle with right hand and left ankle with left hand. Exhale and slowly lower chest to left thigh and hold for six seconds. Repeat on opposite leg.

42

SIDE-TO-SIDE GROIN

Spread your feet beyond shoulder width. Reach outside of your right foot with both hands (Ill. 42), drag hands across the ground to the outside of the left foot. Continue the motion back and forth for five repetitions.

43

FOUR-WAY LUNGE

Stand with your hands on hips and feet together. Step laterally to the right until your thigh is parallel to the ground. Return to the starting position and lunge forward with your right leg. Again, return to the starting position and lunge to the left; return to the start and lunge straight ahead (Ill. 43). Repeat the sequence five times.

STANDING QUAD

Stand erect. Flex one leg and raise the foot to the buttocks as you slightly flex the supporting leg. Exhale, reach down, grasp the raised foot with one hand, and pull your heel toward your buttocks. Hold for six seconds, relax, and repeat three times on each leg.

INCHWORM

Assume a push-up position. Walk your feet toward your hands while keeping both knees straight. When your body forms a triangle, bend one knee and keep the other one straight. Press the heel of the bent knee to the ground and hold for six seconds. Repeat the process three times on each leg.

OUTFIELD SPRINTS (PRE-GAME WORKOUT)

Twenty minutes. Perform two 60–80 yard sprints, sprint 30–40 yards in reverse, rest and repeat.

FLEXIBILITY

BOTH KNEES TO CHEST

Bring both knees to chest and hold. Then slide palms around soles of the feet, interlace fingers, and hold.

ONE KNEE TO CHEST

Bring right knee to chest and hold for 10 seconds. Then pull knee across chest to opposite shoulder and hold for 10 seconds. Repeat with left leg. This exercise helps relieve tightness in the lower back, buttocks, and groin.

EXTEND KNEE: HAMSTRING

Bring one knee to chest, slide hand behind knee, and extend leg straight up. Relax and repeat three times for each leg.

LOWER-BACK STRETCH

Cross right leg over left knee and gently push left knee toward the floor with the right leg (Ill. 44). Repeat on the opposite side. Then place right hand under left knee and pull knee across chest to right shoulder and hold (Ill. 45). Repeat on opposite side.

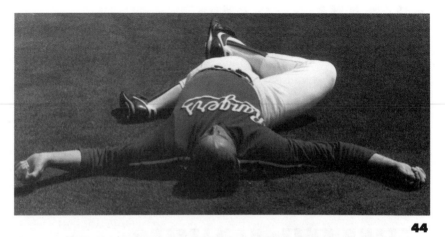

44

45

BACK TWIST

Sit with the left leg straight. Bend right leg and cross right foot over left knee. Rest left elbow outside of right knee, look over right shoulder, and twist upper body to the right (Ill. 46). Repeat on the opposite side.

46

47

GROIN STRETCH

Place soles of feet together, elbows on knees and hands around toes or ankles. Push down on knees with elbows and hold (Ill. 47). Remove elbows from knees, bend forward, and pull head toward toes.

SEATED HAMSTRING STRETCH

With right leg straight, bend left knee and place left foot against inside of right thigh. Bend forward at hips, grasp ankle, and hold. Repeat with left leg (or perform with both legs straight ahead of you (Ill. 48).

48

49

SEATED THIGH STRETCH

Sit with left leg bent, heel outside of left hip and toes straight behind the leg, not turned to the outside (Ill. 49). Bend right knee and place sole of foot inside the left thigh. Lean backward and hold. Repeat for the right leg.

SEATED V-HAMSTRING STRETCH

Sit upright on the floor with legs spread wide apart. Keeping both legs straight, extend the upper back, rotate and lower trunk to one knee and hold (Ill. 50).

Repeat to other knee and then bend forward at the waist and lower trunk to the ground (Ill. 51).

BENT-OVER HAMSTRING STRETCH

Walk hands from toes to heels, keeping knees straight (Ill. 52).

52

HURDLER'S TWIST

From the previous position, rotate at the waist and alternately touch opposite hand to opposite foot.

PLOUGH

Lie on your back and bring both feet over your head until they rest on the ground behind the head. Alternately bend and straighten the knees (Ill. 53). Then alternately raise and lower the legs with knees straight.

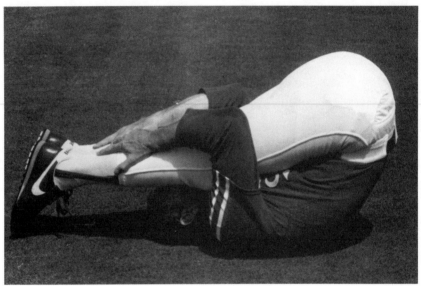

53

INCHWORM

Assume push-up position. Walk feet toward hands keeping both knees straight. Walk through hands and stand upright.

ARM CROSS

With elbows bent, slowly cross the arms in front of the body at shoulder height. Gradually extend the arms at the elbows and increase the intensity of the crosses until you are throwing the arms across the chest as vigorously as possible to assure maximum stretch.

ARM CIRCLES

Make complete circles with the arms, both forward and backward.

54

LATERAL BENDING

Bend to the right 10–15 times and then repeat to the left (Ill. 54). Always bend laterally before bending forward.

LATERAL LEG RAISE

Lie on your back, extend your right leg out in front of you, grasp the sole of your left foot, and bring your left leg behind you, feeling the stretch in your hamstring (Ill. 55). Hold and repeat with the other leg.

55

ARM THRUST (UP AND BACK)

Throw the arms up and back over the tops of the shoulders as vigorously as possible.

TORSO TWIST

Stand erect with knees slightly bent, upper arms extended and parallel to the ground and hands up. Rotate the body to each side.

PUNCH AND ELBOW

Twist to the left and extend the left arm behind the body as if elbowing someone behind you. At the same time, extend the right arm as if punching someone in front of you. Repeat to the right.

HEEL-TO-TOE ROCK

From the squat position, extend both knees, keeping hands on the ground. Push up on the toes and hold. Then rock back on the heels and hold. Rock back and forth from heels to toes five times and hold.

SQUAT

Place feet slightly wider than shoulder-width apart. Squat until thighs are parallel to the ground. Place palms flat on the ground with hands inside knees. Hold for 10–20 seconds.

ANTERIOR-POSTERIOR GROIN (TWO PARTS)

Part 1: Place the left leg ahead of the right with the right knee about one inch off the ground and the front leg at a 45-degree angle. Lower your hips and hold for 6–10 seconds (Ill. 56). *Part 2:* Drop right knee to the ground, place both hands on left knee, keep trunk erect, and slowly slide right knee backward and hold. Repeat on the other side.

56

HANGING HAMSTRINGS (4 POSITIONS)

Position 1—With feet slightly wider than shoulder-width apart, cross hands behind back and lean forward at the waist—hold for six seconds. *Position 2*—Fold arms across the chest and continue to hang for six seconds (Ill. 57). *Position 3*—Let arms drop straight to the ground and continue to hang for six seconds (Ill. 58). *Position 4*—Reach behind right knee, pull chin to knee, and hold. Walk hands down to ankle and hold. Repeat on left side.

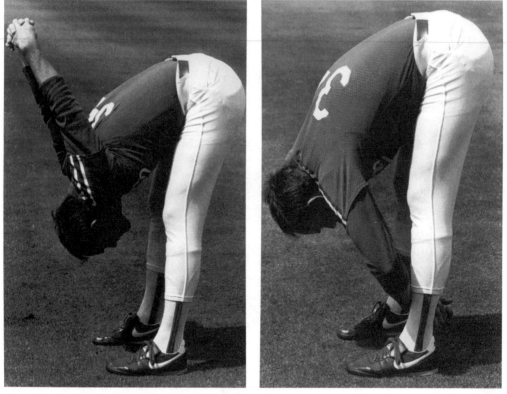

57   58

SHOULDER STRETCH (CROSS-CHEST)

From a kneeling position, extend the right arm straight in front of the body. Grasp the right elbow with the left hand, slowly pull the arm across the chest and hold for 10 seconds (Ill. 59). Repeat with arm up across the nose and down across the waist. Repeat with left arm.

59

•

PHYSICAL CONDITIONING

•

TRICEPS STRETCH

With arms overhead, place the right hand across right shoulder and rest it on the center of the back below the neck. Hold the elbow of the right arm with the left hand and gently pull the elbow behind the head and hold for 10 seconds (Ill. 60). Repeat with left arm.

60

SHOULDER STRETCH (DOWN AND BACK)

Place the left hand across the left shoulder and rest it on the center of the back below the neck. Place the right hand behind the back with fingers pointing upward, palm away from the back. Inch the top hand down and the bottom hand up, trying to interlock fingers. Repeat to opposite side.

SHOULDER STRETCH (SEATED)

Sit on the floor with your arms extended shoulder width behind your back; your palms are on the floor. Slowly inch your feet and lower body away from your hands to stretch the muscles across the anterior chest and shoulders (Ill. 61). Hold for 10 seconds; relax and repeat three times.

61

FOREARM STRETCH

Kneel with palms flat on the floor, fingers toward your knees. With palms flat, lower buttocks toward heels. Can also be performed from a standing position (Ill. 62).

62

LOWER-BACK VARIATION

Place your palms flat on the floor and pull your body forward with your hands while pushing your buttocks to the rear over the feet (Ill. 63). Hold the stretch and repeat.

63

HIGH KICK

From a standing position, hold right arm forward at shoulder height. Swing left leg upward across body and kick right hand five times. Repeat with right leg.

Cross-Training Applications

Throwing the football. That's what Tom House's program is probably best known for. I wondered about this practice when I first signed with the Rangers. It was something I didn't want to rush into.

I spent the first few months of the 1989 season getting my arm in shape. I figured I'd give the football a try when I was good and ready. I eased into throwing it, had positive results, and slowly became a believer in its value.

The football is now an important part of my program. I'll toss it around before a start to loosen up my arm. By doing that I feel like I don't have to throw as many warm-up pitches.

Tom knows more about this procedure than I do, so I'll let him explain.

Using footballs in a baseball environment is an example of cross-training: improving performance in your sport of choice by participating in a different—yet relevant—physical activity.

The concept is really quite simple: Muscles, tendons, ligaments, and bones all support the specific movements of varying sports, especially those that involve throwing and striking skills, in exactly the same way. Dr. Anne Atwater, a researcher at the University of Arizona, was the first to champion this view.

What you're asking of your body when throwing a football, then, is identical to what you're asking of your body when throwing a baseball. This cross-training model applies equally to volleyball, tennis—even swimming.

That's why Nolan Ryan's program is appropriate and beneficial for any athlete: Nolan's lifts, stretches, and abdominal exercises prepare the participant for the physical requirements of his skill, regardless of the implement he uses.

Consider the biomechanical similarity between a pitcher and a volleyball player. A pitcher is subject to the forces of deceleration on the shoulder capsule after the landing leg hits the ground and the baseball is released. Deceleration places much of the stress on the rear deltoid muscle—remember there are three muscle groups that accelerate the arm and only two that decelerate the arm. Nolan's program is designed to address this natural imbalance by adding muscle strength and endurance to the shoulder via weight training.

A volleyball player's shoulder receives a similar form of mechanical abuse: His arm accelerates rapidly unti it makes contact with the ball. Then, at the point of impact, the arm slows down abruptly and the shoulder is forced into jarring deceleration. At least a pitcher doesn't have to worry about impact; his only concern is release and then deceleration. But, of course, a pitcher has the additional strain of pitching off of an elevated mound.

Two different sports, both requiring strong and resilient shoulder muscles. A volleyball player using Nolan's program can balance muscle strength and muscle endurance, from front to rear, to steer clear of disabling injuries.

Baseball players striking volleyballs, football players throwing baseballs, even tennis players throwing footballs—the skills are complementary; the corresponding weight-training needs are virtually identical.

Charlie Hough, the most mechanically efficient pitcher I've ever seen, is a classic example of cross-training in action: Charlie is a proponent of throwing the football. He was a quarterback in high school—a pretty good one—and that helped him establish a firm base of near-perfect mechanics as a pitcher. Every time Charlie threw a spiral, his arm muscles memorized the correct mechanical alignment of pitching a baseball.

Throwing a football is akin to throwing a baseball, except for one thing—a football weighs 13 ounces. So in the ½ mass ×

velocity squared formula for establishing workloads for a pitcher's training program, all you have to do is replace 5 ounces with 13 to devise a comparable program for football players.

Tennis players, particularly guys who hit really hard like Andre Agassi, could learn a thing or two from Nolan's dedication to conditioning. Force applied on the back, shoulders, and arms during the tennis serve should be offset in the weight room.

The only distinction between pitching a baseball and serving a tennis ball is that you have a 2½-foot racquet taking the place of a pitcher's fingertips at release point. In fact, putting topspin on a tennis ball duplicates the same palm, wrist, and forearm angle as throwing a curve or a slider with a baseball.

Swimmers also fit the cross-training formula—stylists in the breaststroke and butterfly require comparable upper-body muscle strength to pitchers and quarterbacks. A swimmer's movement through range of motion in the water enlists chest, shoulders, arms, and back—much like Nolan and Joe Montana. A swimmer is lucky, though, that he doesn't have to worry about problems of deceleration or impact.

Nolan Ryan is the consummate cross-trainer—he prepares in the weight room for the physical demands of pitching; he rehearses the mechanics of his art by throwing the football. Any athlete following Nolan's program will enhance his skill and conditioning base—23 years of success don't lie.

THROWING

I believe that the young pitchers of today don't reach their maximum physical potential because they're overprotected; they're regulated so they don't throw enough fastballs between starts and in games. They don't get the opportunity to learn what

they're actually capable of doing as far as stamina and conditioning are concerned.

Preparation through conditioning is the key to increasing your velocity and handling the stress of throwing a lot of fastballs. An exercise and conditioning program builds a base of strength, but you need to throw between outings to get your arm ready for the wear and tear of competitive pitching.

My career demonstrates how the game has changed in its approach to throwing. When I first came up with the Mets it was all left up to the individual; I just pitched off a mound between starts, delivering as many pitches as it took to feel loose and mechanically sound. I didn't follow a specific throwing schedule; remember, in those days I had no set spot in the rotation, so I never knew when I was going to pitch next. No one was protecting me—they just put me out there and had me throw the fastball. With the Angels, I had to adjust my throwing to the demands of a four-man rotation: I'd pitch off of a mound for 8–12 minutes (going through my full repertoire) on the second day after a start. The idea was to loosen up the arm, get over the stiffness from the last outing, and work on the mechanics of the delivery. I wanted to throw until I felt ready to go into a game, but not to the point that it would jeopardize the integrity of my next start. Of course, the first and third days were set aside for rest and recovery.

With the Houston Astros, where we generally had five starters, I was given a choice between throwing on either the second or third day after a start. My usual pattern was to throw off of a mound for 8–12 minutes on the third day, with some long toss on the second day.

Long toss—a game of catch with a gradual increase in the distance between the two participants—is an important part of Tom House's throwing program with the Rangers. Two guys start playing catch about ten yards from each other, then stretch it out a little, slowly increasing the distance until you're 60–70 yards apart. The goal is to throw the ball on a perfect line, never missing the target. I'd played long toss with the Mets, Angels, and Astros, but not to the extent that I now do with the Rangers. Here's my current throwing pattern between starts.

Day 1: I'll toss a football for 10–15 minutes to get my arm loose. Usually, I'll throw it at progressively longer intervals, leading up to a distance of 25–30 yards. The football helps me recover from the strain of pitching; it warms up the arm while relieving any residual stiffness and soreness.

Day 2: Again, I throw a football for 10–15 minutes (working up to a distance of 25–30 yards). After I'm completely warmed up, I'll play long toss for 10–15 minutes, then I'll pitch on flat ground—at a distance of 52–54 feet from the catcher—for 10–15 minutes. I'll work on all my pitches, from both the windup and stretch, before calling it a day. Flat-ground work allows you to fine-tune your delivery without falling prey to the tearing-down process of throwing off of an elevated mound (in fact, I've added it to my off-season program).

Day 3: I'll loosen up with a football for 10–15 minutes, then pitch off of the mound for 10–12 minutes. By the end of this interval I feel comfortable with all of my pitches, ready to throw a good ballgame. The flat ground work on Day 2 enables me to spend less time on the mound on Day 3, while ensuring that my delivery will be consistent and in synch for the next start.

Day 4: Rest.

After the Rangers play their last game, I go home to Alvin for the winter to take care of my ranch and the cattle operation. No throwing until January—that's my rule, as it takes a while for the body to recover from a long season.

January 1–15: I start throwing a football and playing long toss

about 3–5 times per week, just long enough to warm up the arm.

January 15–31: Time to add flat-ground work for 8–12 minutes every other day (time permitting).

February 1: I'll start throwing off of a mound for 10–15 minutes every other day, getting the feel of all my pitches, to prepare for my arrival at Port Charlotte, Florida, on March 1.

Off-season throwing depends on the weather and how my arm is responding; I believe in a flexible approach. Basically, I follow my Day 1 in-season program (plus long toss) for two weeks, add Day 2 (on January 15) and complement the conditioning with a Day 3 in-season session (on February 1). This way I know I'm going to be ready when the first exhibition game rolls around.

Pitching is a job, one that demands preparation, hard work, and repetition—both in the weight room and out on the field. In my earliest days as a high school hurler in Alvin, I threw hundreds of fastballs per game and per workout; it was my bread and butter, the only way I knew how to pitch. All those fastballs, both in high school and in the minors, trained my arm to handle the stress of throwing the heater.

Young pitchers need to use more discretion in favoring breaking balls and other off speed pitches over fastballs. If you don't throw your fastball enough, then it's not going to improve.

A pitcher's conditioning and his mechanics are of great importance to longevity. If you have proper conditioning at a young age, then you can overcome bad mechanics for a certain period of time; what that period of time is, mind you, I don't know. But every pitcher with bad mechanics must face a turning point— the crucial stage when the aging process overrides your conditioning program. Then it's essential to develop proper mechanics or you'll be through. Sound mechanics and exercise can reduce your risk of injury while increasing your chances of longevity.

●

**PHYSICAL
CONDITIONING**

●

Most injuries occur when people fatigue. Much less common are the freak injuries—you trip, you slip, you run into somebody while trying to make a catch. Conditioning cannot overcome freak injuries, but it will often prevent fatigue-related injuries.

Pitching with correct mechanics puts less stress on your body; conditioning gives you more stamina. You'll be able to go farther down the road and you'll get into less of a deficit.

I've certainly benefited from good mechanics and a solid conditioning base. But I haven't fallen victim to the aging process like a lot of other people. Many of the guys I broke in with could have prolonged their careers if they'd had a better attitude about nutrition, exercise, and mechanics. I'm not saying they would have pitched into their forties, but they might have added two or three good years to their career.

Genetics have played an important role in my success. Throwing a great fastball is a combination of genes, coordination, and timing—qualities that cannot be taught. You can't take a person without the genetic potential to throw a fastball and somehow work miracles—the guy who could do that would make all kinds of money. You're born with raw talent; it's up to you to refine it and make it work to your advantage.

Most hard throwers are tall guys with big hands. I'm an exception. My hands are not that big, so I choke the ball when I throw a fastball—I grip the ball really tightly and put it in the back of my hand. Pitchers with large hands—such as Sandy Koufax—throw the fastball more off the fingers.

The bigger the hand, the better the leverage, and leverage produces greater velocity. Take guys like Jim Bibby and J.R. Richard, for instance. They didn't have particularly good arm speed, but their size enabled them to throw hard because of the leverage they put on the baseball. Their fastball would just explode in on the hitter.

Good genes are a plus. But you also need to look at what types of pitches a guy throws throughout his career. I believe, and I have nothing but intuition to back this up, that people who throw

sliders lose their velocity more quickly than people who don't. As they get older, and their fastball slows down, they tend to rely more on the slider. The slider takes away from their velocity. And before too long, their velocity—and the sharp slider along with it—is gone. Instead of following the natural way to put force on the ball, they try to create additional rotation by using their wrist. I've seen this happen many times.

Another source of early retirement is mental burnout—a pitcher loses his intensity; he's no longer willing to make sacrifices; the game doesn't mean as much to him as it did; it becomes routine.

I can't perform successfully unless my mental attitude is on track. I have to be aggressive and concentrate on getting the job done. It's a challenge I enjoy. For some athletes, though, the mental part of the game wears thin. They just say, "My body is failing me and I have to work too hard—it's not worth all the effort."

I'm a positive person. I really believe that's helped me last as long as I have. I enjoy the game of baseball, with all its ins and outs. But baseball isn't everything.

My cattle operation requires a lot of energy—it's a second full-time business. I never bring baseball home with me, brooding over it and letting what happens in a game dominate my thoughts. And my family makes everything else in my life worthwhile. Being involved in their activities and concerns is very important. It puts pitching in perspective.

It's tremendously satisfying that I've pitched long enough to throw six no-hitters. The last one with the Rangers was really special because it came so late in my career. But all the no-hitters wouldn't mean anything without my family being there to support me. I think you need to seek a sense of balance in your life. Being a complete pitcher is easier and more satisfying if you're a complete person. Work to get the most out of your ability and there's no reason why you can't find success and fulfillment—both as a pitcher and as a human being.

●

PHYSICAL CONDITIONING

●

THE COMPLETE WORKOUT
(In-Season)

DAY 1 Pitching Day	DAY 2	DAY 3
Pre-Game Stretching	Stretching	Stretching
Pre-Game Strength Training**	Strength Training*	
Outfield Sprints	Running/Aerobics	Running/Aerobics
	Abdominal Workout	Abdominal Workout
	Light Dumbbell	
Warm-up Throwing	Throwing	Throwing

*Reduce poundage to 70 percent of maximum during the season.
**Pre-game Strength Training is a single set performed with very little weight.

THE COMPLETE WORKOUT
(Off-Season)

MONDAY	TUESDAY	WEDNESDAY	THURSDAY
Stretching		Stretching	
Weight Training*		Weight Training*	
Light Dumbbell		Light Dumbbell	
Running/Aerobic		Running Aerobic	
Abdominal Workout		Abdominal Workout	
Throwing**		Throwing**	

*Reduce poundage to 85 percent of maximum in January to prepare for spring training.
**Begin to throw on flat ground in January; no pitching off of a mound until February 1.

DAY 4	DAY 5	DAY 1 Pitching Day
Stretching	Stretching	Pre-Game Stretching
Strength Training*		Pre-Game Strength Training**
Running/Aerobics		Outfield Sprints
Abdominal Workout		
Light Dumbbell		
Throwing		Warm-up Throwing

FRIDAY	SATURDAY	SUNDAY
Stretching		
Weight Training*		
Light Dumbbell		
Running/Aerobic		
Abdominal Workout		
Throwing**		

A Pitcher's Diet

How and when you eat have great impact on athletic performance. You should understand the processes your body goes through in the breaking-down and rebuilding stage. Only then is it possible to devise an ideal sports nutrition program.

My diet compensates for what I, as an athlete, ask from my body. By being sensitive to my nutritional needs, I'm better prepared to pitch long and hard in the heat of Arlington, Texas. A proper diet goes hand in hand with endurance and stamina. I've learned this lesson through more than 23 years of major-league experience.

When you work on your diet you'll feel stronger and enjoy eating even more than before. And you'll realize that, hey, nutrition does play a role in conditioning; it's essential to good health and a sense of well-being.

Following a sensible diet, though, is an evolutionary process. A lot of changes have occurred since I was growing up in Alvin. But one thing has remained the same: My mother was a believer in balanced meals, and so am I.

Roasts, potatoes, and vegetables were standards in those days. Steak was a rarity. The Ryan family adhered to a fairly regular meal schedule. We never ate a big supper on Saturdays; everyone was off doing different things on the weekend. But Sundays we'd come home from church and eat fried chicken—that was the big meal of the day. On Sunday evenings we'd make do with leftovers or soup and a sandwich, just something light. My mother really worked as a homemaker and put a lot of effort into preparing wholesome meals. She taught me the basics of good nutrition.

By the time I signed with the Mets, of course, I'd fallen into the fast-food habit typical of young kids. That stuff is inexpensive and convenient. But I always did try to eat properly. I searched out restaurants that offered luncheon specials geared toward a balanced diet.

●

**A
PITCHER'S
DIET**

●

I was really skinny in the late 1960s, a fact not lost on the Mets' front office. They were always encouraging me to gain weight. I think that's why I ate a lot more dairy products and rich foods than I do now.

Things change. I was traded to the Angels and the whole fitness craze burst on the scene. There was more written about diet—what to eat and what not to eat—it was the subject of many TV talk shows and magazine articles. Everyone started running and becoming more weight-conscious.

Reacting pretty much the same way as the general public, I modified my diet by reducing the amount of fats in favor of grains, vegetables, fruits, and nuts. And I also ate more chicken and fish.

Jimmy Reese, a close friend of mine and my mentor when I played for the Angels, was really into nutritional supplementation. Bee pollen, kelp, you name it. I went through a period when I tried quite a few different supplements. I'm always open to new information.

I'm convinced that sound nutrition depends on the good food you put on your table. Now the only supplements I go with are vitamin E and CO-Q-10, an enzyme that Tom House recommends for improving digestion. I'll take one of each with my breakfast, but that's all I take as far as supplements are concerned.

The 1970s came and went, providing both good and bad input on diet. My diet is much better now than it was in the '70s. I'm not as open to fad diets—trends that run their course and don't have any lasting value.

I owe a lot of what I've learned to Gene Coleman. During my stint with the Astros, Gene and I often discussed diet and sports nutrition. He probably had more impact on my eating habits than anyone else. Gene taught me about hidden calories and hidden fats; he made me more aware of what I was eating and the effect it was having on my performance. And he explained

that it's better to eat more often, and in less quantity, than to consume two or three huge meals a day.

When I'm trying to get down to my playing weight of 210 pounds I'll restrict caloric intake—especially from fat and protein—and eat small carbohydrate meals every couple of hours. This approach prevents overeating at mealtime and eliminates the need to binge.

If I'm just maintaining my playing weight and following a regimen of three meals a day, then the key is eliminating all fatty snack foods. I prefer to snack on fruit for quick energy, rather than potato chips, cookies, or candy.

I don't keep an exact calorie count anymore, but my maintenance program calls for 2,500–3,000 calories per day. And, naturally, I'm carefully monitoring where those calories are coming from. On average, here's the split by nutritional category:

50 percent carbohydrates

30 percent protein

20 percent fat

Moderation is essential to good nutrition. I believe in moderation in everything I do.

A balanced diet from the four food groups—now there's a nutritional plan that's hard to beat. And breakfast is probably the most important meal of the day.

A Nolan Ryan breakfast is high in carbohydrates and fiber and very low in fat; it often accounts for one third of my daily calories. Orange juice, black coffee, toast or muffins, some type of cereal and fruit, often of the citrus variety, is what I enjoy in the morning. But I try not to eat the same breakfast two days in a row. In fact, I'll rotate my breakfasts every three days because it's healthier to vary the foods you eat; this wards off food allergies and other health problems.

●

A PITCHER'S DIET

●

Here's a typical three-day breakfast rotation:

Day 1
Pancakes
Whole wheat toast (no butter)
Cantaloupe
Black coffee
Orange juice

Day 2
Oatmeal
English muffin (no butter)
Peeled orange
Plain yogurt
Black coffee
Orange juice

Day 3
Two poached eggs
Raisin toast (no butter)
Grapefruit
Black coffee
Orange juice

A few comments on my breakfast selections:

1. I seldom eat breakfast meats. Some people get the idea that Texans are into bacon, sausage, and the like. Not me, though. I'm quite conscious of fat intake, have been for years. Take a good look at bacon or sausage and all you see is fat.

And to make matters worse, breakfast meats are generally fried in their own grease. Fried foods are bad for your cardiovascular system. I won't touch them. Cut these fatty meats out of your diet and it will really lower your cholesterol level and reduce your daily percentage of fatty calories.

2. I try not to use butter on my bread. And this applies to lunch and dinner as well. My objective is to reduce my caloric intake by eliminating fat-calorie foods.

As mentioned earlier, I limit fat to 20 percent of my total calories—ideally, 40 grams is the upward level of daily animal-

fat consumption. Calculate how much fat a product contains by using the figures on the label. Multiply the grams of fat by nine—the number of calories a gram of fat contains. That gives you total calories from fat. Then look at the number of calories per serving and check to see what percentage of that comes from fat.

Dining out, of course, throws a curveball into this equation. But a simple rule is to order foods grilled, baked, and broiled—not fried. And avoid rich, cream-based sauces.

Stay abreast of hidden fats and read labels—that's what I do. Food is full of surprises. What you don't know *can* hurt you.

3. I enjoy eating yogurt at breakfast. Sure, it's high in calories, but those calories come mostly from sugar, not from fat. Sugar in the morning isn't necessarily bad for you; it's a simple carbohydrate and an effective source of energy. But fruit sugar (fructose) is much healthier than the sucrose found in candy bars and other sweets.

4. Don't eat eggs too often. The yolks are full of fat, though they're also rich in protein. I probably eat eggs once a week—if possible, I have them poached rather than fried or scrambled in butter.

5. Yes, I like pancakes, but not necessarily on the day I pitch. Pancakes don't bring me luck or anything like that. If it's convenient and I'm in the mood, I'll eat them. But I'm not into taking the time and trouble to fix them at home.

Lunch is really variable. During the off-season, when I'm on a normal routine, I'll usually eat a light meal like soup, salad, and a sandwich. Fruit is another staple of my lunch table. I guess you could say that I eat more fruit than anything else. I'm big on melons and citrus—an excellent natural supplier of vitamin C.

The baseball schedule dictates a flexible approach to lunch. If I have a business appointment, for instance, I'll eat out, mak-

●

**A
PITCHER'S
DIET**

●

ing quite sure to order a sensible meal. I might have a grilled piece of chicken for protein, and broccoli or another green, leafy vegetable for fiber and carbohydrates. But much will depend on the starting rotation.

I don't like to pitch on a full stomach. I want to feel light and energetic, not bogged down with heavy food that's hard to digest. The hotter it is—and Arlington, Texas, reaches upward of 100 degrees at game time—the more you experience that sense of discomfort.

Carbohydrates—pasta, fruits, and vegetables—are ideal before pitching. Again, I favor the green, leafy vegetables because they're rich in fiber. I shun cream sauces on my pasta: tomato sauces are so much lower in calories and fat.

And I might have a bowl of soup, but never one made from a cream-based stock. Nothing tastes better than a cream soup, but unfortunately, the cream is laden with fat. I prefer vegetable stocks, occasionally a chicken broth is okay, too, but chicken soups are often high in salt.

The day after pitching is a rebuilding process. Protein replaces carbohydrates as my principal source of nutrition. My body craves the calories it burned while pitching, so I'll treat myself to a nice steak and a baked potato.

Dinner also depends on my spot in the starting rotation and the Rangers' schedule. The same rule applies to dinner as to lunch: Carbohydrates on the day you pitch; protein the day after. But I'll usually eat my biggest meal of the day in the afternoon (two to three hours prior to my late-afternoon workout) because of all the night baseball we're forced to play in Texas.

I don't enjoy eating my main meal late at night after the game. Yeah, there's a big spread of food waiting for us in the clubhouse. I'll check it out and pick and choose based on what looks good. But I'm very selective. I'll pass on peanut butter (too much fat and salt), fatty meats, and salads covered in mayonnaise (because of the oil).

The bottom line is that eating before bed is unhealthy. The food sits on your stomach; you can't burn the calories productively, forcing you to store them as fat; and a full stomach affects your sleep.

After a night game at Arlington Stadium, though, I'll go out for a meal with my family. Just a light snack like a sandwich and soup or salad. This is an opportunity to wind down after the game, put things into perspective, and enjoy a special social occasion as a family. Besides, it keeps me from going to bed dying of hunger—that's almost as bad as sleeping on a full stomach.

During the off-season I'll usually eat dinner at 6:00 P.M.; again, it's a chance to be together as a family. We'll usually eat a balanced meal from the four food groups.

I really enjoy those family meals, a rewarding break from the regular routine of a big-league pitcher. If that pitcher also happens to lift weights, as I do, then the nutritional cycle becomes even more complicated.

As a morning weight trainer I set the alarm to allow ample time for a light breakfast 90 minutes prior to my workout. I don't believe in lifting on an empty stomach; this is a sure way to get lightheaded or dizzy—at least, that's been my experience. But eating too close to a training session promotes nausea and discomfort. So I wake up early enough to eat breakfast, read the newspaper, relax, get dressed, and head to the weight room— it's an important ritual.

When we're on the road I'll call room service and ask them to deliver my breakfast early. I just check off that selection card and leave it on my door. Normally, there's no problem. Sometimes, though, a travel day or an afternoon ball game forces me to eat breakfast at 5:30 A.M. and lift at 7:00 A.M.

I never think twice about getting out of bed at the crack of dawn to eat breakfast before my workout—my training is an essential element to my success and longevity. Some days I don't feel like getting up so early, but it's worth the extra effort to stay in shape.

My body has undergone many changes in the past few years. Proper nutrition is an ally I rely on to slow the aging process. But there's nothing I can do to alter the fact that I sweat a lot more now than I did early in my career. My metabolism just doesn't function on the same level as it did when I was younger.

But whether you're 44 or 14, fluid loss is still a major concern. The last thing any pitcher needs is to be dehydrated. I always drink lots of water before taking the mound. And I'll add to that pre-game hydration regimen by drinking water every half inning, as well as at the end of the game.

Water is superior to any beverage that contains sugar—it takes longer for your body to break down the sugar and incorporate the liquid into your system. So I just like to drink straight, pure water.

In Arlington, due to the extreme heat, we'll take electrolytes to combat dehydration. Tom recommends a product called Joggers's Juice, a little packet of electrolytes that prevents a depletion of fluid.

Dehydration promotes cramping and exploits any strength imbalances in your body. I know that when my fluid levels go down, for instance, my old hamstring injury creeps up and it's hard to pitch. I believe in maintaining fluid levels to keep ahead of these problems. You can't wait until you have a deficiency to address the disorder; you have to stay on top of your game at all times.

The
Complete
Pitcher

6

Many people attribute my strikeouts to sheer velocity, the Nolan Ryan fastball at work. Well, the fact is that if you see high strikeout totals—if I'm in double figures when you check a box score—it means I'm throwing my curveball for a high percentage of strikes.

Gene Coleman charted every single pitch I made for the Astros. His research proved that when I throw breaking balls for strikes it translates into strikeouts and success. Getting my curves over for strikes early in the game sends a message to the hitters—they have to think about the breaking ball. And it gives me the confidence to throw the curve in the later innings, in those game-on-the-line situations when I really need it.

Earlier in my career, before I developed a consistent change-up, throwing strikes with the curve was even more crucial. If the curve wasn't working I was a one-pitch pitcher, and a guy with only one pitch is destined to struggle.

The change-up provides me with another option. Now, if I get behind in the count and I don't have a good breaking ball, I can go to the change. It's especially helpful if I'm throwing it for strikes and the hitter is expecting a fastball.

Changing speeds is part of a pitcher's repertoire. A change-up, for instance, needs to be 15 mph slower than a fastball. Ten mph below the fastball is okay, but only if the pitch is low and in the strike zone. Low means down around the knees.

The whole purpose of the circle change—my particular style—is to force a hitter to transfer his weight out in front so he can't drive the ball; instead, he'll usually hit on top of the ball.

It's a reasonably easy pitch to learn, but requires time and patience to master. Here's how I got started throwing it:

It was the first day of the baseball strike in 1981. The Astros flew into New York to prepare for a series if, in fact, the labor issues could be resolved. The Cincinnati Reds had just wrapped

●

THE COMPLETE PITCHER

●

up a set with the Mets and were staying at our hotel. It was an off day for both clubs, and everybody was hanging around in the coffee shop, just waiting to hear whether the strike was going to come off.

I ran into Joe Nuxhall over breakfast. He'd been a Reds' broadcaster for years. Somehow we got to talking about Mario Soto; he had the best change-up in baseball at this point. I asked Nuxhall about Soto's grip and he demonstrated it to me: You take your index finger and curl it up inside your thumb. You don't use your index finger to grip the ball; it's the other three fingers that hold the ball. So you're actually making a little circle with your hand alongside the ball as you throw the pitch.

I'd never seen anybody throw a ball like that before. I flew home after the strike became official and started playing catch while using the grip. Then, when the season started again in August, I experimented with the circle change in game situations. I used it enough to gain a measure of confidence. The more I threw it, the more it developed and improved. I don't think it really came around until 1985 or so, but it has been a big factor in my success the last couple of years.

The circle change is an asset in 3–2 situations. When I ran the count to 3–2 in the early '80s with the Astros, I was throwing strictly fastballs. Hitters were aware of my pattern, comfortable knowing they were sure to see a fastball. And they'd end up fouling off an awful lot of strikes. I might walk a hitter after throwing eight or nine pitches.

I have confidence in my fastball. I'm not afraid to throw it 3–2, regardless of whether a guy is waiting on it or not. But I will also throw a change on 3–2 to keep a hitter honest. If you make sure the pitch is down, a batter might chase it, even if it's out of the strike zone.

My pitch selection varies with the count. On 2–0 I'll go with a fastball or change. An 0–2 count calls for a curve or fastball, depending on the hitter. In general, I usually throw about

65–70 percent fastballs. But my ratio of fastballs to curves to change-ups will depend on the stuff I have that day. Is my fastball low or high 90s? Am I getting my curveball over for strikes?

I think the curveball is the hardest pitch to throw consistently. It breaks down and away due to rotation and spin. You're always trying to throw it in the lower quarter of the strike zone, a narrow target with a small margin for error. And this makes it hard for umpires to call the pitch accurately; it is, without a doubt, the toughest pitch to call.

Pitchers who throw their curves up in the strike zone are effective until they tire or hang one. The result? They get hurt by giving up a big hit or home run. Bert Blyleven is a good example. He has an excellent curveball and will throw it up in the strike zone a lot, but you can tell by the number of home-run balls he's thrown that he gets beat on that high curve.

My big problem isn't hanging the curve; it's my tendency to struggle with both control and rhythm in the first inning. Two factors could account for this problem.

Power pitchers, more than anyone else, have trouble moving from bull-pen mounds to game mounds. All mounds are different, and it's often difficult for a hard thrower to adjust his mechanics and feel to the different angle of a game mound.

Then you have what I call the adrenaline factor. It's a proven fact that you could put the radar gun on a guy warming up to go into the game and he thinks he's throwing as hard as he can—maybe 87, 88 mph on the speed gun. All of a sudden you put a hitter in the batter's box under game conditions and the pitcher will throw three to four mph faster. This is pretty much true of all pitchers, not just a select few.

So you look at those factors, pencil them into the equation, and it comes out that many guys—like me—will take longer to make the adjustment when they start a game. Getting into a good groove in the first inning is tough.

My goal is to escape the first inning without giving up any runs, establish the tone of the game, gain the confidence of my teammates, and build my own confidence. It's important to feel you're in a groove, have control of your pitches, and sense that everything is in order.

I'd like to complete every game. If I'm fatiguing, though, I'll tell the manager to get the bull pen ready. I'm not going to let ego influence my good judgment. My job is to give our team an opportunity to win—that's all you can ask of a starting pitcher. But a starting pitcher can't fall too far behind early in the game or it will demoralize his teammates.

I had big problems in the first inning with the Astros in '83 and '84. Gene Coleman checked the stats and discovered that if I allowed the leadoff man to reach base, then he'd score 60 percent of the time. That's why I work so hard to prevent the leadoff man from getting on.

A successful pitcher keeps the leadoff hitter from reaching base and puts the first pitch over for a strike—the two most important rules of pitching. The first pitch doesn't even have to be as good as the others, since many hitters are looking for a ball in a certain zone. If they don't get it, they'll lay off and take a strike.

Boggs and Mattingly often take the first pitch. They check you out, analyze what you're throwing. And then if you miss—according to their reasoning—they'll even get a better pitch to hit the next time around.

Effective pitching requires adaptation and intelligence. You can't get by with one pitch, even if that pitch is a 98-mph fastball. The curve and change transformed me from a thrower to a complete pitcher. Learning how to pitch opened the door to the special moments of a long and satisfying career.

STATISTICAL ANALYSIS

Every pitch thrown by Nolan Ryan while a member of the Houston Astros was clocked for velocity and recorded for type, location, ball/strike, etc. Between 1980 and 1988, data were recorded in 134 games in which he threw approximately 30,000 pitches. The following is a summary of the data:

Total pitches 27,918

Strikes 17,505 (62.7%)

Fastballs 17,309 (62%)

  Strikes 11,597 (67%)

  Average velocity 93.76   (90–99)

                                                  (no fastball below 90)

Curveballs 6,421 (23%)

  Strikes 3,236 (50.4%)

  Average velocity 78.30 (66–83)

Change-up 7,538 (24%)

  Strikes 4,809 (63.8%)

  Average velocity 82.30 (71–89)

Average velocity by inning

1: 93.7	6: 94.0
2: 94.1	7: 94.4
3: 94.1	8: 94.6
4: 94.4	9: 94.5
5: 94.1	10: 94.0

Average velocity by year

1980: 95.1	1983: 94.7	1986: 93.5
1981: 95.0	1984: 94.5	1987: 93.3
1982: 94.9	1985: 94.1	1988: 93.3

Opponents' batting average (1980–88)

Total	Fastballs	Curve	Change-up	2-Strikes
.215	.213	.182	.265	.135

Note: Struck out batter 53% of time with two-strike count. Threw first-pitch curve 24% of the time; only 3% were put into play.

Source: Gene Coleman, Houston Astros.

The Sixth No-Hitter, June 11, 1990

It was one of those nights when everything just seemed to go my way: The fastball was really good—I could put it wherever I wanted—and I had the change-up working. My curveball wasn't at its best, but the other two pitches took the pressure off; I'd just show the curveball to a hitter to make him aware of it.

I can't say I had any early signs that it was a no-hitter type of game. You never know about something like that. I just tried to stay focused on getting ahead of the hitters, challenging them with my fastball, and keeping them off-balance by throwing the change-up.

You can't become distracted by the fact that you've got a good game going and haven't given up any hits. That can turn around on you really quick. I recall a game against Cleveland when I was still pitching for the Angels. I took the mound in the seventh inning with a no-hitter. Three pitches later I'd given up three home runs. I had no explanation for that happening; I just made three bad pitches.

I've been in the no-hitter situation quite a bit, often enough to know not to be distracted by the whole thing. You just don't think about it. You look up in the sixth inning and you haven't given up any hits. The fans start sensing it. Guys start acting different in the dugout, though they don't say anything. You try to make good pitches and win the ball game—that's all you can do.

The Oakland A's are so explosive. There was no way I could get comfortable, even after Julio Franco hit his second home run of the game to pad the lead a little. Sure, Jose Canseco was out with his back problem. Mark McGwire had been struggling and was given the night off. But that put two new guys—Dave Jennings and Felix Jose—in the lineup. And frankly, it's harder for me to prepare for hitters I haven't faced before.

Rickey Henderson was my number one concern. I've had reasonably good success against him, but the kind of hitter he is, well, he's always going to battle you, do anything he can to

reach base. In other words, he won't swing at any bad pitches. But I got ahead in the count against him and that kept me out of trouble.

Having my son Reese in the dugout during the game was a special treat. Given all the back problems I had in 1990, he was worried my back would stiffen as the game went along. He came over in the seventh and asked me how my back felt and started rubbing it. I think he was nervous and didn't know what to do with himself.

The other guys on the team pretty much left me alone, as will happen when you're pitching a no-hitter, but Reese kept rubbing my back, patting my leg—that helped relax me. As the game was nearing its end, I just continued to block all that no-hitter stuff out of my mind. I know from experience that the last six outs are the toughest.

When it was all over, I had a great sense of satisfaction. Ruth, my daughter, Wendy, and Reese had been a part of this special night. It's nice any time your family can share in your success.

One thing that makes it so meaningful is that it came at such a late stage in my career and so much time had elapsed between the fifth and sixth (no-hitters). Because of that, and all the near misses, I think this one means more to me than maybe the others did.

Reflections on Longevity

Longevity varies with each person. Certain athletes are going to age more quickly than others whatever they do, and that's a function of genetics.

Why do some people live longer? Well, if they die of natural causes you could say that genes are the determining factor. You look at a family in which everyone lives into their nineties, and then you see another family where they all pass away in their sixties and seventies. Yeah, it's genetics and, of course, environmental issues come into play as well.

The older you get, the more you realize that the background your parents instilled in you has a direct effect on what you do in life and how you go about doing it. And so I'm a believer that people are products of their environment. I'm not saying you can't change, but I honestly think your environment affects how much you're capable of accomplishing.

In other words, through physical conditioning, a good diet, and the right attitude you can actually slow down the aging process. You can't deter the body from aging, but you can slow the pace at which it ages.

A pitcher's conditioning and his mechanics are of great importance to longevity. If you have proper conditioning at a young age, then you can overcome bad mechanics for a certain period of time; what that period of time is, mind you, I don't know. But every pitcher with bad mechanics must face a turning point—the crucial stage when the aging process overrides your conditioning program. Then it's essential to develop proper mechanics or you'll be through. Sound mechanics and exercise can reduce your risk of injury while increasing your chances of longevity.

Most injuries occur when people fatigue. Much less common are the freak injuries—you trip, you slip, you run into somebody while trying to make a catch. Conditioning cannot overcome freak injuries, but it will often prevent fatigue-related injuries.

Pitching with correct mechanics puts less stress on your body; conditioning gives you more stamina. You'll be able to go farther down the road and you'll get into less of a deficit.

I've certainly benefited from good mechanics and a solid conditioning base. But I haven't fallen victim to the aging process like a lot of other people. Many of the guys I broke in with could have prolonged their careers if they'd had a better attitude about nutrition, exercise, and mechanics. I'm not saying they would have pitched into their forties, but they might have added two or three good years to their career.

Genetics have played an important role in my success. Throwing a great fastball is a combination of genes, coordination, and timing—qualities that cannot be taught. You can't take a person without the genetic potential to throw a fastball and somehow work miracles—the guy who could do that would make all kinds of money. You're born with raw talent; it's up to you to refine it and make it work to your advantage.

Most hard throwers are tall guys with big hands. I'm an exception. My hands are not that big, so I choke the ball when I throw a fastball—I grip the ball really tightly and put it in the back of my hand. Pitchers with large hands—such as Sandy Koufax—throw the fastball more off the fingers.

The bigger the hand, the better the leverage, and leverage produces greater velocity. Take guys like Jim Bibby and J.R. Richard, for instance. They didn't have particularly good arm speed, but their size enabled them to throw hard because of the leverage they put on the baseball. Their fastball would just explode in on the hitter.

Good genes are a plus. But you also need to look at what types of pitches a guy throws throughout his career. I believe, and I have nothing but intuition to back this up, that people who throw sliders lose their velocity more quickly than people who don't. As they get older, and their fastball slows down, they tend to rely more on the slider. The slider takes away from their velocity. And before too long, their velocity—and the sharp slider along with it—is gone. Instead of following the natural way to put force on the ball, they try to create additional rotation by using their wrist. I've seen this happen many times.

THE TOP-TEN STRIKEOUT VICTIMS (THROUGH THE 1990 SEASON)

1. Claudell Washington 39
2. Fred Patek 31
3. Jorge Orta 30
4. Larry Hisle 29
5. Rod Carew 29
6. Amos Otis 27
7. Andre Dawson 26
8. Al Bumbry 24
   Carlton Fisk 24
9. Dale Murphy 23
10. Darrell Porter 23

Source: Texas Rangers.

These guys all fit the same basic profile: free swingers who didn't walk much and hit up in the order. And they all chased the curveball—I'd throw a good curveball and they'd lunge after it, expecting the fastball.

Rod Carew is on the list, but he hit .300 against me; when he made contact, the ball had a funny way of dropping in. Andre Dawson is very much a free swinger. But when he's hot there's no stopping him—he'll even hit a ball that's thrown over his head.

I honestly think that Jose Cruz, whom I managed to strike out twice when I pitched for the Mets, was one of the toughest hitters in the National League. There wasn't a single pitch he couldn't handle. Pitch him in and he'd bloop it to left. Pitch him down and in and he might hit a line drive down the right-field line for a double. Jose was a great hitter and a real asset to the Astros when we played together in the '80s; I'm glad I never had to face him in his prime.

Another source of early retirement is mental burnout—a pitcher loses his intensity; he's no longer willing to make sacrifices; the game doesn't mean as much to him as it did; it becomes routine.

I can't perform successfully unless my mental attitude is on track. I have to be aggressive and concentrate on getting the job done. It's a challenge I enjoy. For some athletes, though, the mental part of the game wears thin. They just say, "My body is failing me and I have to work too hard—it's not worth all the effort."

I'm a positive person. I really believe that's helped me last as long as I have. I enjoy the game of baseball, with all its ins and outs. But baseball isn't everything.

My cattle operation requires a lot of energy—it's a second full-time business. I never bring baseball home with me, brooding over it and letting what happens in a game dominate my thoughts. And my family makes everything else in my life worthwhile. Being involved in their activities and concerns is very important. It puts pitching in perspective.

It's tremendously satisfying that I've pitched long enough to throw six no-hitters. The last one with the Rangers was really special because it came so late in my career. But all the no-hitters wouldn't mean anything without my family being there to support me. I think you need to seek a sense of balance in your life. Being a complete pitcher is easier and more satisfying if you're a complete person. Work to get the most out of your ability and there's no reason why you can't find success and fulfillment—both as a pitcher and as a human being.

Nolan Ryan's Minor- and Major-League Pitching Totals

Year	Club	W-L	ERA	G	GS	CG	ShO	SV	IP	H	R	ER	BB	SO
1965	Marion	3-6	4.38	13	12	2	1	0	78	61	47	38	56	115
1966	Greenville	17-2	2.51	29	28	9	5	0	183	109	59	51	127	272
	Williamsport	0-2	0.95	3	0	0	0	0	19	9	6	2	12	35
	New York (NL)	0-1	15.00	2	1	0	0	0	3	5	5	5	3	6
1967	Winter Haven	0-0	2.25	1	1	0	0	0	4	1	1	1	2	5
	Jacksonville	1-0	0.00	3	0	0	0	0	7	3	1	0	3	18
1968	New York (NL)	6-9	3.09	21	18	3	0	0	134	93	50	46	75	133
1969	New York (NL)	6-3	3.54	25	10	2	0	1	89	60	38	35	53	92
1970	New York (NL)	7-11	3.41	27	19	5	2	1	132	86	59	50	97	125
1971	New York (NL)	10-14	3.97	30	26	3	0	0	152	125	78	67	116	137
1972	California	19-16	2.28	39	39	20	9	0	284	166	80	72	157	329
1973	California	21-16	2.87	41	39	26	4	1	326	238	113	104	162	383
1974	California	22-16	2.89	42	41	26	3	0	333	221	127	107	202	367
1975	California	14-12	3.45	28	28	10	5	0	198	152	90	76	132	186
1976	California	17-18	3.36	39	39	21	7	0	284	193	117	106	183	327
1977	California	19-16	2.77	37	37	22	4	0	299	198	110	92	204	341
1978	California	10-13	3.71	31	31	14	3	0	235	183	106	97	148	260
1979	California	16-14	3.59	34	34	17	5	0	223	169	104	89	114	223
1980	Houston	11-10	3.35	35	35	4	2	0	234	205	100	87	98	200
1981	Houston	11-5	1.69	21	21	5	3	0	149	99	34	28	68	140
1982	Houston	16-12	3.16	35	35	10	3	0	250.1	196	100	88	109	245
1983	Houston	14-9	2.98	29	29	5	2	0	196.1	134	74	65	101	183
1984	Houston	12-11	3.04	30	30	5	2	0	183.2	143	78	62	69	197
1985	Houston	10-12	3.80	35	35	4	0	0	232	205	108	98	95	209
1986	Houston	12-8	3.34	30	30	1	0	0	178	119	72	66	82	194
1987	Houston	8-16	2.76	34	34	0	0	0	211.2	154	75	65	87	270
1988	Houston	12-11	3.52	33	33	4	1	0	220	186	98	86	87	228
1989	Texas	16-10	3.20	32	32	6	2	0	239.1	162	96	85	98	301
1990	Texas	13-9	3.44	30	30	5	2	0	204	137	86	78	74	232
	A.L. Totals	167-140	3.11	353	350	167	44	1	2625.1	1819	1029	906	1474	2949
	N.L. Totals	135-132	3.23	387	356	51	15	2	2365	1810	969	848	1140	2359
	Career Totals	302-272	3.16	740	706	218	59	3	4990.1	3629	1998	1754	1614	5308